THE SHAAR PRESS

THE JUDAICA IMPRINT
FOR THOUGHTFUL PEOPLE

THE ENEMY

A
SHAAR
PRESS
PUBLICATION

WITHIN

CONFRONTING YOUR CHALLENGES
IN THE 21ST CENTURY

RABBI ABRAHAM J. TWERSKI, M.D.

Published by **SHAAR PRESS**
Distributed by MESORAH PUBLICATIONS, LTD.
4401 Second Avenue / Brooklyn, N.Y 11232 / (718) 921-9000 / www.artscroll.com

Distributed in Israel by SIFRIATI / A. GITLER
6 Hayarkon Street / Bnei Brak 51127

Distributed in Europe by LEHMANNS
Unit E, Viking Industrial Park, Rolling Mill Road / Jarrow, Tyne and Wear, NE32 3DP/ England

Distributed in Australia and New Zealand by GOLDS WORLD OF JUDAICA
3-13 William Street / Balaclava, Melbourne 3183 / Victoria Australia

Distributed in South Africa by KOLLEL BOOKSHOP
Shop 8A Norwood Hypermarket / Norwood 2196, Johannesburg, South Africa

ISBN: 1-57819-763-5 Hard Cover
ISBN: 1-57819-764-3 Paperback

Printed in the United States of America by Noble Book Press
Custom bound by Sefercraft, Inc. / 4401 Second Avenue / Brooklyn N.Y. 11232

ৰ্঳ Table of Contents

Introduction

"**G**-d maintains a war against Amalek from generation to generation" (*Exodus* 17:16).

Virtually all of Torah literature describes our sojourn on earth as an ongoing struggle. For reasons known only to His Divine wisdom, G-d created man with many strivings and urges which we are expected to direct into the proper channels. He commanded us to curb some of them, and to avoid others. He also commanded us to do many things, some of which we have a natural tendency to resist. As Job said, "Man is born to toil" (*Job* 2:7).

The Torah writings describe this as a struggle between two opposing forces: the *neshamah*, a Divine soul which innately desires to fulfill the will of G-d, and a *yetzer hara*, a force which acts to deter us from fulfilling the will of G-d. This confrontation begins with the earliest onset of our ability to reason and continues throughout our entire lifetime.

Engaging in battle is neither easy nor pleasant. Much energy must be expended to avoid being vanquished by the enemy, and one may be wounded in the process. Soldiers on the front know that they are always at risk. They must maintain a constant state of alertness to defend themselves, and they must seek ways to defeat the enemy.

Periodically, a soldier leaves the front for a period of rest and recreation (R & R), only to return to the battlefield. It is obvious that his duty is to do battle against the enemy, and the intervals of "R & R" are intended to restore his physical and emotional energies. No one thinks that the soldier is at the front primarily for periods of "R & R."

This is equally true of our battle against the *yetzer hara*. We do have moments when we can partake of and enjoy the goods of the world, but we should see these as periods of "R & R." These should not distract us from the primary obligation to triumph in our battle.

Much of Western civilization views the world as an amusement park. If people do not receive what they think is their fair share of enjoyment, they may feel shortchanged. "The world has not been nice to me. It has not given me what I so justly deserve."

But what if the world was not created to be an amusement park? What if everything in the world was *not* put there just to serve our needs? What if it is just the other way around — that we were put here to do something for the world, the *tikun olam* of which so many people speak but relatively few people do? The emphasis shifts completely. No one owes us anything. It is *we* who are obligated, and we owe the world something.

This is not the prevailing view in Western civilization, which is essentially hedonistic, and try as we might to avoid it, we are subject to this influence. Rambam states that a person is profoundly influenced by his environment, and recommends that if one cannot find an appropriate community, one should retire to the wilderness rather than be subjected to an ethos that is antithetical to Torah (*Hil. Dei'os* 6:1).

I do not know where, in Western civilization, we can find a

community that is immune to the prevailing culture. Realistically, it is not feasible to retreat to the wilderness. We must live in a community where there are educational facilities for our children as well as other resources for basic Jewish needs.

We are left with only one option: *maximizing* our capabilities to wage a successful battle against the *yetzer hara*.

R' Eliyahu Lopian cites the Talmud that the reason all living things, including animals, were destroyed in the flood is because even the animals had become perverted (*Sanhedrin* 108a). He asks: What sense does it make to punish animals? They do not choose to do good or evil.

R' Lopian states that just as in the physical world bacteria can infect all they come in contact with, this is also true in the spiritual realm. Degenerate behavior by humans infects and poisons the environment, so that everyone and everything becomes infected and contaminated. The animals were not destroyed because they were sinful. Animals do not sin. They were destroyed because they had been corrupted by the widespread degenerate and sinful behavior of humans. Those that were saved by Noah, the Talmud says, had not become perverted.

(Recent history helps us understand this. Governments destroyed many millions of livestock because some animals had become infected with foot-and-mouth disease. This was not a punishment, but a necessity to eliminate a source of disease.)

If we realize the moral decadence which prevails in our time, we can understand the enormity of the risk we face of being contaminated by our environment. One may say, "I cannot be expected to put forth effort in Torah like the Chafetz Chaim or the Gaon of Vilna did." The fact is that we today must make *greater* efforts than did the *tzaddikim* of previous generations. They lived in a far less toxic environment.

We are fortunate in having an extensive literature, with hundreds of volumes written over the past two millennia about the struggle with the *yetzer hara*. But in these writings it is frequently stressed that the character of the battle changes from generation to generation. "G-d maintains a war against Amalek from generation to generation" (*Exodus* 17:16). Amalek is the personification of evil. The war against evil changes from generation to generation.

When weapons were bows and arrows, shields were an adequate defense. When the attacker uses tanks, the defense is an antitank gun. And when the weapon is a nuclear missile, antimissiles must be used.

Furthermore, not only are the *yetzer hara's* weapons different and more formidable, but we have become weaker fighters. R' Itzele of Petersburg points out that because recent generations have become physically less robust, halachic authorities have given broader exemptions from fasting. It is even more evident, he says, that in comparison with the spirituality of previous generations, we are much weaker (*Kochvei Ohr*, p.41). We must find additional armamentaria to combat the *yetzer hara*.

Techniques that were effective in the *shtetl* may not be adequate for a metropolis. Methods that sufficed years ago are insufficient in the days when the media spew violence and graphic immorality. Given the unprecedented lack of ethics and morals that prevails today, new battle techniques may be necessary. Much of the traditional material is relevant, but needs to be presented in a manner that would make it effective in our time.

The classical works of *mussar* are fundamental to living a Torah life. *Duties of the Heart (Chovas HaLevavos), The Ways of the Righteous (Orchos Tzaddikim) The Path of the Just (Mesilas Yesharim)* and *Making a Personal Inventory (Cheshbon HaNefesh)* are basic readings. However, in each generation, Torah scholars have found it necessary to add to them. Contemporary ethicists, R'Eliyahu Dessler (*Michtav M'Eliyahu*), R' Shlomo Wolbe (*Alei Shur*), R' Chaim Shmulevitz (*Sichos Mussar*), R' Avraham Pam (*Atarah LaMelech*) and others, with their perception of contemporary problems, elucidate the principles of *mussar* for us.

R' Dessler cites the phenomenon that just before a candle extinguishes, it may have a spurt of flame. It is a common experience that when a combatant feels he is about to be vanquished he makes one last effort, mustering whatever strength remains. Now that we are approaching the ultimate Redemption, which will mark the end of Satan's powers, he is making one last stand to corrupt people. This is another reason why our generation must take additional steps against the *yetzer hara's* machinations.

We are fortunate in having many people who begin the day with *daf yomi* (Talmud study), and this is certainly commendable. However, Talmud study can be an intellectual exercise which may not affect a person's behavior. Listen to what R' Chaim Yosef David Azulai (Chida) says.

> There are some Torah scholars who do not wish to learn anything other than Talmud and halachah, and do not wish to learn *mussar*. For the greater part, they are vain about their scholarship and consider themselves to be very wise . . . Those scholars that have fear of G-d in their hearts should hasten to learn *mussar*, and then their Torah study will be meritorious" (*Devash Lefi, Taf*, 21).

Some people who are meticulously Torah observant may feel that they have no need to learn *mussar*. They may think, "What can I do over and above that which I am already doing?"

It is related that the Gaon of Vilna, whose knowledge of Torah was encyclopedic and whose performance of mitzvos were as near perfection as attainable by a human being, would learn the second chapter of *Mesilas Yesharim* (Path of the Just) *thirteen times* before venturing into the street. Our knowledge of Torah and performance of mitzvos are light years distant from that of the Gaon, and the streets we venture into are much more toxic and decadent than the streets of Vilna. Logically, we should read that chapter of *Mesilas Yesharim* at least twenty times before leaving the house. How many people read it even once?

Even powerful weaponry is not sufficient in battle. Intelligence is necessary to know what are the enemy's plans, where does he plan to strike, and with what force. It is helpful to know who his generals are, and what are their theories of warfare. When possible, a preemptive strike may be advisable.

I must draw upon material that I have heard or read over the past sixty years. Wherever possible, I will provide my sources. However, there are many thoughts whose sources I do not remember.

Anyone familiar with my writings knows that I also draw upon my clinical experience for concepts that I have learned working with people struggling with emotional disorders. Some of the techniques that have been found effective in overcoming psychological problems may find application in the struggle to maintain spiritual health.

The struggle with the *yetzer hara* is unrelenting. As Rabbeinu Bachya says in *Duties of the Heart*, "You may be asleep, but the *yetzer hara* is always alert" (*Yichud HaMaaseh*, chap. 5).

We can use every bit of help in this formidable battle. I hope that this book will contribute to our arsenal.

1

Just What *Is* the *Yetzer Hara*?

The *yetzer hara* is not a simple entity.

In our morning prayers we say: "Are not all the heroes like nothing before You, the famous as if they never existed, the wise as if devoid of wisdom and the perceptive as if devoid of intelligence? For most of their deeds are desolate and the days of their lives are empty before You. *The pre-eminence of man over beast is non-existent, for all is futile*" (*Ecclesiastes* 3:19). Some *siddurim* continue with, "Except for the pure soul, which is destined to give a reckoning before You."

In other words, a human being is a composite creature, comprised of an essentially animal body and a Divine soul.

This reminds me of something I heard from one of my recovering patients. He said, "My ego cries for perfection. But honesty tells me that I am human, that humanity is not so terrible, and that it's okay to be "half child of G-d and half animal."

This is not correct. While we may start out in life as "half child of G-d and half animal," it is *not* okay to stay that way. Our goal is to transform the "animal half" to become G-dly.

Animals were created with a mission to behave according to their nature. Man was indeed given an animal body, but his Divine soul enables him to become master over the animalistic drives and channel them into actions that will enable him to fulfill his mission for which he was created. Failure to exercise this mastery reduces man to an animal level.

The drives that are inherent within our animal-like body comprise part of the *yetzer hara*. All the drives of an animal are self-centered, seeking only gratification. Animals have hunger, envy, rage and lust. These drives are present in humans as well, and the *yetzer hara* seeks their gratification.

It is important to know that although a person can and should become master of these drives and channel them appropriately, he cannot extirpate them, and they remain with him throughout life. This is why there can never be a let-up in the struggle with the *yetzer hara*. If we let our guard down, these drives can emerge. They are an integral part of a human being.

According to *Tanya*, there were very few people in our history who were able to totally dispose of their innate drives. This requires not only an extraordinary effort in the service of G-d, but also a special Divine gift, whereby G-d removes that which is beyond a human being to do.

The Chafetz Chaim would go to the *beis midrash* (Torah study hall) in the early hours of the morning. Several of his students concealed themselves under benches to see what the *tzaddik* was doing. They saw the Chafetz Chaim open the *Aron Kodesh* (Ark housing the Torah Scrolls), and tearfully plead with G-d to take away his feelings of anger.

No one ever saw the Chafetz Chaim angry. He was always in total control of his reactions. However, the *feeling* of anger when one is provoked is not under voluntary control. Just as it is natural to feel pain when one is seared by a hot iron, so it is natural to feel anger when one is provoked. Only G-d can remove a natural feeling, and it is for this that the Chafetz Chaim was praying.

In addition to the drives which are clearly animalistic, the human being has many ego drives, most of which probably do not exist in animals. These, too, are part of the *yetzer hara.*

The above drives comprise the *internal yetzer hara*, which is an integral part of every human being. There is also an *external yetzer hara*. This is Satan, an angel whom G-d created to offset the forces of *kedushah* (holiness). Whereas the internal *yetzer hara* simply seeks gratification of internal drives, Satan operates with determination to fulfill his mission: to deter people from doing G-d's will.

Satan is a formidable foe. I will borrow a term that is used by people recovering from alcoholism. They say, "We must be aware that alcohol is our enemy, *cunning, baffling and powerful.*" This is how we should think of Satan: an unrelenting enemy, who is cunning, baffling and powerful. Consequently, not only must we be on constant alert against his wile, but we must also be aware that not only does Satan exploit the internal *yetzer hara* for his purposes, he also uses a variety of tactics to achieve his mission. Just as in a war, it is not only necessary to have an arsenal equivalent to that of the enemy, but one must also be able to "out-general" the other side.

It is important that we be aware that the struggle with the *yetzer hara* is relentless. The Rebbe of Kotzk said that one should always conceptualize that the *yetzer hara* is holding an axe over a person, threatening to sever his head. One chassid asked, "What if I cannot visualize that?" The Rebbe answered, "That indicates that your head has already been severed." The *yetzer hara* may delude us into thinking that we have already subdued it. If we give up the battle, the enemy wins.

It is for this reason that Torah literature contains so many volumes of instruction on the battle against the *yetzer hara.* A cunning enemy will not continue to use a battle plan that has failed, but will constantly develop new strategies to over-power the adversary. This book contains information and advice on how to conduct the battle with the *yetzer hara* that is using advanced weapons and new tactics of war.

R' Yitzchak Blaser (R' Itzele of Petersburg) states that whereas the *yetzer tov* and the *yetzer hara* are equal in strength, there is a significant difference. The *yetzer hara* operates spontaneously. The body's cravings do not have to be activated. The *yetzer tov*, however, is in *potential*, and it must be activated in order to be functional. This is why the Talmud says that a person must provoke the *yetzer tov* against the *yetzer hara* (*Berachos* 5a).

While the *yetzer hara's* strength and tactics are formid-able and constitute a major challenge, we should realize that we will have Divine assistance in subduing it. Furthermore, G-d will do the lion's share of the work, but we must initiate it.

A man described his internal struggles as, "I have two dogs inside of me, constantly fighting with each other."

"Which one wins?" he was asked.

"Whichever one I feed," he responded.

We can nourish the *yetzer tov*, or we can nourish the *yetzer hara*. Whichever one we feed will triumph.

R' Simchah Zissel cites the verse when Moses saw the burning bush, "I will turn aside and look at this great light" (*Exodus* 2:22), upon which the Midrash says, "R' Yochanan said that Moses took three steps toward the bush. Resh Lakish says that he turned his head toward the bush. G-d said, 'Because you made the effort to see, I will reveal Myself to you.' " Moses' incomparable greatness began with just the minutest effort. This, said R' Simchah Zissel, is what is meant by the Midrash, "G-d says, 'Open for Me a passageway like the eye of a needle, and I will open for you portals that can be traversed by wagons' " (*Shir HaShirim Rabbah* 5).

R' Mendel of Kotzk commented, "Yes, an opening as tiny as the eye of a needle is all that is necessary to invoke G-d's assistance, but the opening must penetrate the personality through and through. It cannot be superficial."

We can achieve the upper hand in the battle against the *yetzer hara* by taking even a tiny step in the right direction, but it must be taken with the utmost sincerity.

Let us now proceed to examine some of the *yetzer hara's* weaponry and strategies, both historical and current.

The *Yetzer Hara's* Goal

B efore discussing the *yetzer hara's* methodology, let us consider just what it is that it wishes to accomplish.

As mentioned, Satan was created to offset the effects of *kedushah*. *Kedushah* results when man fulfills the purpose for which he was created: to do the Divine will, which, the Gaon of Vilna says, is primarily the refinement of *middos*. Using the force of the *yetzer hara*, Satan is out to thwart that achievement, and will use any tactic for that purpose, no holds barred. One opinion in the Midrash says that the angel that wrestled with the Patriarch Jacob (*Genesis* 32:25) was the patron angel of Esau, and appeared to him disguised as a *tzaddik*, in the attempt to deceive Jacob into thinking that he was a friend.

The goal of the yetzer hara is to deter a person from Torah or so disable him that he cannot fulfill his mission on earth.

> *A chassidic rebbe once entered the beis midrash (Torah study hall) and ran through the aisles as if in pursuit of someone. He finally fell upon the bookcase of sefarim, then said to his chassidim, "The yetzer hara was here,*

and I tried to catch him, but he eluded me by hiding among the sefarim." In other words, the yetzer hara may disguise itself as if it wishes to encourage Torah study.

The Chafetz Chaim would come into the yeshivah study hall late at night and send the students to bed. "The drive to stay up late at night to study Torah is not the work of the yetzer tov. It is the yetzer hara that wishes to deprive you of adequate sleep so that your mind will be dull tomorrow." With this he interpreted the evening prayer, "and remove Satan from before us and behind us." The Chafetz Chaim said, " 'Before us' is understandable. We ask that Satan should not be an obstacle to our doing mitzvos. But what does 'behind us' mean?

"It means," the Chafetz Chaim said, "that sometimes Satan stands behind us and pushes us as if to do more mitzvos. 'Stay up all night and learn. Fast regularly as atonement for your sins. Don't limit your tzedakah to the 20 percent limit stated by halachah. Give more and more, even if you impoverish yourself.' By urging us to excesses, it may drain our energies and resources, ultimately incapacitating us so that we cannot observe Torah and mitzvos."

R' Elchanan Wasserman said that although the yetzer tov never oversteps its boundaries, the yetzer hara does. If it is to its advantage, the yetzer hara will push a person to do "mitzvos"; i. e,, what it considers to be a mitzvah. For example, the yetzer hara suggests that it is important to bring Jews into the synagogue to pray and to hear words of Torah. Therefore, the synagogue should be made most inviting to accommodate more people. The mechitzah (separation) between men and women should be removed. People who live far from the synagogue should be allowed to drive on Shabbos. "Mitzvos" such as these are the counsel of the yetzer hara.

Sometimes it is not clear whether what appears to be a mitzvah is indeed so, or is a ruse of the *yetzer hara.* R' Elchanan says, "Beware of a mitzvah that has wide popularity. Check with a halachic authority whether this is in fact a mitzvah."

R' Elchanan cites several incidents in the Torah. When donations for building the Sanctuary were sought, only *"Everyone whose heart motivates him"* donated (*Exodus* 35:5). When they sought gold for the Golden Calf, *"The entire people removed the gold rings that were in their ears"* (*Exodus* 32:3). When the Israelites were to receive the Torah, *"Moses brought the people forth from the camp toward G-d"* (*Exodus* 19:17). They did not come forth on their own. When they wanted to send spies to Canaan, *"All of you approached me and said, 'Let us send men ahead of us and let them spy out the Land' "* (*Deuteronomy* 1:22). When it came to praise G-d for the salvation from Egypt, *"Then Moses and the children of Israel sang' "* (*Exodus* 15:1). When the spies returned from Canaan with a negative report, *"The entire assembly rose up and issued its voice; the people wept that night"* (*Numbers* 14:1).R' Elchanan commented, "When it is for something good, you don't find 'everyone, all the people, the entire assembly' rushing to do it. Widespread enthusiasm for what appears to be a mitzvah should cause one to be on the alert" (*Lekach Tov, Deuteronomy* vol.1 p. 45).

How alert one must be that the *yetzer hara* may be urging a mitzvah can be seen from the following story.

> The Chafetz Chaim related that when R' Chaim of Volozhin wished to establish a yeshivah, he sought counsel from his mentor, the Gaon of Vilna. The Gaon gave him no response, and R' Chaim left empty handed.
>
> After several years, R' Chaim felt that the yeshivah was absolutely essential, and again consulted the Gaon. This time, the Gaon promptly gave his approval. R' Chaim asked, "Why did the master not approve of this last time?"

The Gaon replied, "Your reasons for establishing the yeshivah were as valid then as now. However, you were so fired up with passion and enthusiasm that I was suspicious that the yetzer hara might have been involved. Pure mitzvos usually do not provoke such passion. Now that you are presenting it with a more serene demeanor, I think it is an excellent idea" (ibid.).

That the *yetzer hara* may lead a person to sin by masquerading as a *tzaddik* is further evident from an incident related in the Talmud. During the period of the Second Temple there were times when people exploited Torah for selfish goals. The Talmud warns us against this: "Improperly used, the Torah can be turned into a deadly poison" (*Yoma* 72b).

Two *kohanim* (priests) were competing for the privilege of performing part of the service in the Temple, and one stabbed the other to death (*Yoma* 23a)! Think of it! What is a most abhorrent act was seen as an acceptable way to serve G-d. That is how deceptive the *yetzer hara* can be.

The Talmud proceeds to make an important psychological comment on this tragic incident. It relates that the father of the victim, finding that his stricken son was still alive, exclaimed, "My son has not died, and the holy utensil has not become *tamei* (impure by contact with a dead body)." The Talmud denounces the father saying, "It was not the zeal for the holy utensil that led to his comment, but the cheapening of the value of human life."

Man's charge is to elevate oneself spiritually, to become closer and ultimately unite with G-d. The vehicle for this is observing the mitzvos, as the Torah states, "To love G-d, to listen to His voice and to cleave to Him" (*Deuteronomy* 30:20). The Talmud explains that one can cleave to G-d by becoming more G-dlike, emulating G-d. "Just as He is merciful, so you shall be merciful. Just as He is slow to anger and forgiving, so you should be slow to anger and forgiving" (*Shabbos* 133b).

The only way this closeness to G-d can be achieved is by listening to G-d's voice and cleaving to Him; i.e., refining one's *middos* (character traits). It is noteworthy that man's first sin resulted when the *yetzer hara*, in the form of the serpent, told Adam that if he would eat the forbidden fruit he would be "like unto G-d" (*Genesis* 3:5). The cunning of the *yetzer hara* was in not disputing man's goal to emulate G-d. Rather, it suggested an alternate and easier way to do it. No need to struggle to transform one's character traits. Just eating this fruit will make you "like unto G-d." The *yetzer hara* has never relinquished this tactic of enticing a person to do wrong by convincing him that it is right. *Deluding a person to see things differently than they are in reality or to think that what is wrong is right is one of the yetzer hara's powerful tactics.*

That refinement of *middos* is man's goal is evident in the Midrash, "The mitzvos were given for no reason other than to refine people" (*Vayikra Rabbah* 13:3). Inasmuch as refinement of *middos* is man's ultimate goal, the primary attack of the *yetzer hara* is to debase one's *middos*. Here the external *yetzer hara*, Satan, utilizes the internal *yetzer hara*, which is a person's desire to gratify the physical drives. If he can cause a person's inborn traits to remain at their undeveloped, animalistic level, he has triumphed.

Listen to the words of the sage, R' Aharon Kotler, who cites the Midrash, "If a Torah scholar is bereft of good sense, a dead carcass is better than him" (*Vayikra Rabbah* 1:15). R' Kotler says, "If there is a lack of proper behavior, all one's Torah learning is worthless ... because the Torah was given to man *only after he achieved the human perfection as it applies to middos*" (*Mishnas R' Aharon* 1:135).

One may ask, "But is not Torah study the means to achieve character refinement? After all, the Talmud quotes G-d as saying, 'I created the *yetzer hara*, and I created Torah as its antidote" (*Kiddushin* 30b). Then Torah study is of value before one has achieved refinement of *middos*. It is the vehicle whereby one can refine one's *middos*."

Make no mistake about it. Torah study is supreme, as the Mishnah says, "Torah study is equivalent to the sum total of many mitzvos" (*Peah* 1:1).

R' Eliyahu Lopian explains this. Torah study can indeed help a person transform his character traits, *but only if he wishes it to do so* and studies Torah with that intent. Simple Torah knowledge not directed to refinement of *middos* accomplishes nothing (*Lev Eliyahu* vol. 1 p.74).

This concept is echoed by R' Shlomo Wolbe, who points out that the *berachah* we recite each day for the study of Torah is that "He commanded us to be engaged in Torah." R' Wolbe cites the Midrash (*Shir Hashirim Rabbah* 8), "Do not despise one another, envy one another or embarrass one another, lest the heavenly angels say to G-d, 'The Torah You have given to the Israelites, *they are not engaged in it*, since there is dislike and envy between them.' " Regardless of how much people may study Torah, if their *middos* are not refined and they have aversion and envy for one another, they are *not engaged* in Torah (*Alei Shur* vol.1 p.29).

R' Lopian cites the Torah account of the Patriarch Abraham sending Eliezer to his birthplace to find a wife for Isaac, and making his trusted servant take a solemn oath that he would not take a woman from the Canaanites. Eliezer knew that a girl who would evidence the trait of *chessed* (acts of kindness) would be appropriate for Isaac.

"But," R' Lopian asks, "why was *chessed* adequate? After all, growing up in a pagan environment, with a family of idol worshipers, would that not disqualify her? Why would a girl from a pagan family be preferable to a Canaanite?"

R' Lopian states that the Canaanites were corrupt in *middos*, and there was no way they could ever come to accept the true G-d. *If a person has noble middos, then exposure to the truth will enable him to realize the truth of G-d.*

That is why Eliezer felt that a girl with *middos* of *chessed*, when taken away from a pagan environment and brought into the home of Abraham, will readily manifest *yiras shomayim* (reverence for G-d).

R' Lopian quotes R' Chaim Vital, "The reason the Torah does not specifically dictate *middos* as mitzvos is because they are prerequisites to mitzvos. *One must be more cautious in avoiding bad character traits than even in the observance of the positive and restrictive mitzvos, because with good middos, observance of the mitzvos is easily achieved*" (*Shaarei Kedushah* 2:2. *Lev Eliyahu* vol. 1 pp. 69-70).

The esteemed Torah scholar, R' Chaim Brill, just weeks before his demise, asked a friend to take him to visit a sick person. The friend, seeing R' Chaim's frail condition, was hesitant to do so. R' Chaim said, "I do not have to prepare or even eat before a *shiur* (Talmudic lecture), but I cannot say a *shiur* without having done an act of *chessed.*" The friend took R' Chaim to make the visit.

As noted, the undeveloped traits in man are all self-centered. Overcoming self-centeredness is, therefore, essential to refinement of the *middos*. The Midrash's statement that the function of mitzvos is character refinement was expressed in these words by Rabbi Akiva. " 'Love your neighbor as yourself' is the all-encompassing rule of Torah" (*Jerusalem Talmud* 9:4). The sincere willingness to sacrifice one's own comfort or possessions to help other people is the antithesis of self-centeredness. Empathizing and identifying with another person requires the refinement of *middos*.

How one can refine one's *middos* will be discussed in subsequent chapters.

This is clearly stated in Psalm 15. "*O G-d, who may sojourn in Your Tent? Who may dwell upon the mountain of Your Sanctuary? He that walks in moral integrity and practices righteousness and speaks the truth with his heart. He who has borne no slander upon his tongue, nor done evil to his fellow nor tolerated an aspersion cast upon his neighbor. In whose eyes one who is blameworthy is despised, and he honors those who fear G-d. He has sworn to his detriment and does not change his vow. He who has not put out his money for usury, nor has taken a bribe against an innocent man — he who acts as by these principles will not falter forever."*

In order to fulfill these requirements, a person must divest himself of self-centeredness. It is then that he can dwell in G-d's Tabernacle, having succeeded in emulating G-d and in cleaving to Him.

R' Yisroel of Salant pointed out that the verse in the Torah, "You shall be holy, for I, your G-d, am holy" (*Leviticus* 19:2), is followed by the mitzvos, *"You shall not steal, you shall not deny falsely, and you shall not lie to one another . . . You shall not cheat your fellow and you shall not rob; you shall not withhold a worker's wage with you until morning . . . You shall not commit a perversion of justice . . . You shall not carry gossip. You shall not stand aside while your fellow's blood is shed . . . You shall not take revenge and you shall not bear a grudge. You shall love your fellow as yourself."* It is the observance of these mitzvos that makes a person holy.

One might ask: What is the role of observance of all the ritual mitzvos? The Midrash answers this. "Does it make any difference to G-d in what way an animal is slaughtered? The mitzvos were given for no reason other than to refine people" (*Vayikra Rabbah* 13:3). The Divine wisdom knows that observance of all 613 mitzvos is essential to achieve the all-encompassing rule of "Love your neighbor as yourself."

The *yetzer hara* may say, "Look here. Inasmuch as the goal of the Torah is to love your neighbor and refine your character traits, why, you can do that without observing all the ritual mitzvos. You can be friendly and helpful to people without keeping kosher, can't you? You can develop fine character traits without restricting yourself so stringently on Shabbos."

This is the cunning of the *yetzer hara*. He may present arguments which may appear logical. However, the wisest of all men has forewarned us against falling into the trap of apparently logical arguments. "Do not rely on your own understanding" (*Proverbs* 3:5). "All a person's ways are right in his own eyes" (ibid. 16:2). Whatever it is that you may desire, whether it is to provide pleasure or greater convenience, you are likely to find many ways to justify your actions.

The Talmud says that sins numb a person's feelings (*Yoma* 39a). A person who violates any of the mitzvos loses the sensitivity that is requisite for refinement of *middos*. On the other hand, observance of the ritual mitzvos without refinement of *middos* misses the point.

> R' Michoel Ber Weismandl related that he spent one Succos in Yemen. On the morning before Succos, a man came into shul carrying a large sack, and emptied hundreds of esrogim (citrons) onto the table. Each worshiper picked up an esrog and put a few coins into a tzedakah box.
>
> R' Michoel Ber was taken aback by this. He was accustomed to people checking esrogim with a magnifying glass to detect the minutest defect. The casual acquisition of an esrog did not reflect the esteem one should have for the mitzvah.
>
> The following day, one of the worshippers stood by the pulpit to lead the service, when another worshipper pushed him away from the pulpit, exclaiming, "Yesterday he told a lie, and today he wants to lead in the prayers!"
>
> R' Michoel Ber reflected, "We are indeed fastidious in seeing that the esrog should be without the slightest blemish, but are we equally scrupulous that the chazzan (reader) should be free of a blemish? Perhaps these people have their priorities in proper order."

Speaking of sensitivity and of *esrogim* brings to mind an anecdote of the Chafetz Chaim. One Succos there was a dearth of *esrogim*, and there was only one *esrog* in the entire community. Everyone said the *berachah* for the *esrog*, and when the Hallel was recited, the *esrog* and *lulav were given to the Chafetz Chaim that he might perform the traditional waving of the four species. The Chafetz Chaim refused to accept them, since it might arouse envy and resentment among other scholars. "Waving the four species is only a custom. Having envy and resentment is a much more serious Scriptural transgression" (Atareh LaMelech p. 123).*

R' Yerucham Levovitz cites R' Akiva's statement that "Love your neighbor" is the all-encompassing principle of Torah. He says that "all-encompassing" means that all 613 mitzvos fall under the rubric of "Love your neighbor." Therefore, R' Yerucham reasons, if one's love for others is not enhanced by the performance of a mitzvah, it indicates that the mitvah was lacking in completeness.

Emotions exert a powerful effect on our thought processes and judgment. The Torah says, "Do not take a bribe, because a bribe can blind the eyes of even the wise and can distort even the words of the righteous" (*Deuteronomy* 16:19). Just as a judge loses his objectivity when he is bribed, so do we lose our capacity to make proper judgments when we are "bribed" by our desires. King Solomon states this so emphatically. "There is a way that appears proper to a person, but it is a path to death" (*Proverbs* 14:12). Cocaine addicts have told me that each use of this potentially deadly drug was the result of a judgment that it was the right thing to do at the time. The lethal consequences either did not occur to them or was explained away.

One of the most dangerous and deceitful maneuvers of the *yetzer hara* is to cause a person to feel dejected. The chassidic master, R' Aharon of Karlin, said, "Although the Torah does not explicitly state that being sad is sinful, there is nothing that can bring about as much sin as feeling dejected." Sadness is a very painful feeling, and people may do many unwise things in an attempt to relieve this pain.

The *yetzer hara* may cleverly twist the words of the Talmud that "one should be exceedingly humble" (*Ethics of the Fathers* 4:4) to mean that a person should consider himself inadequate, incompetent and worthless. These negative feelings deprive a person of ambition and the will to do anything. He may think himself too dull to learn Torah. He may be so convinced that he is going to fail that he gives up without trying.

We should at all times be aware of our great worth, as the Talmud says, "Beloved are the people of Israel, for they are described as the children of G-d" (*Ethics of the Fathers* 3:18). Indeed, it is precisely this feeling of great worthiness and pride that should deter us from doing anything that is beneath our dignity.

Several of our ethicists have emphasized the importance of a true self-awareness, not denying one's potential. The Chazon Ish said, "Many people err in understanding humility, thinking that it means to consider themselves dull and incompetent. True humility is to know one's capacities and value ... but not to demand to be honored for these. The awareness of one's talents should stimulate a person to greater achievement in Torah and spirituality" (*Diglenu*, Kislev 5714).

A true self-awareness requires admitting to oneself all one's thoughts and feelings. The ethicist, R' Shlomo Wolbe, shares an extremely important insight with us. He says that when the *yetzer hara* stimulates an improper drive within a person, the person may feel offended that he is capable of so base a feeling. Because his pride is offended by this, he may try to disown the thought. He is more concerned with his ego than with the baseness of the thought.

Disowning the thought does not allow one to master it. It is driven into the subconscious from where it continues to exert its influence. Accepting that one is capable of the thought is like discovering where the enemy is hiding, and one can then take steps to vanquish it. The traditional *mussar* writings instruct us how to overcome improper thoughts and feelings. It is the denial of such feelings that is most dangerous (*Alei Shur* vol.1 p.35).

R' Wolbe makes a very important comment which is most germane to the subject of the problems of our generation.

> "This generation is not similar to previous generations in the study of mussar ... When R' Nosson Zvi Finkel asked R' Yisroel Salant on what principle he should base his yeshivah, R' Yisroel said, 'to revive the spirit of the lowly and to revive the heart of the crushed' (Isaiah 57:15). This was R' Nosson Zvi's mission throughout his entire lifetime, to lift the spirits of Torah scholars ... This generation has descended precipitously in grasping the elevation of man and the greatness of Torah.
>
> "The people of this generation are unable to withstand the sharp rebuke the earlier generations heard from their teachers who were mussar authorities. Furthermore, the analysis of their deeds and middos to discover the baseness in them will crush and discourage the younger generation more than it will wisen them. Only after an extended period of elevation of their spirit and implanting a knowledge of the human greatness will they be able to acknowledge the baseness that is part of man ... It is more difficult to learn one's character assets than to discover one's defects ... Before we can acknowledge the baseness inherent in man we must have a clear understanding of his admirable traits" (Alei Shur vol. 2 pp. 158-159).

If the *yetzer hara* succeeds in driving a person into a state of dejection, it has triumphed. It may even allow him to go through the motions of observing mitzvos, giving him a false sense of security that he has actually vanquished the *yetzer hara.* But if it has drained a person of the *simchah* (joy) in life, it has triumphed. This is evident in the words of Moses, that the sin which results in the greatest hardships is "because you did not serve G-d with *simchah*" (*Deuteronomy* 28:47). R' Chaim Vital explains the great danger in dejection: "Sadness prevents one from observing mitzvos, studying Torah and praying with *kavannah . . . it is the opening which the yetzer hara uses to mislead a person*" (*Shaar Kedushah* 2:4).

Similarly, the *yetzer hara* may allow a person to go through the motions of observing the mitzvos, while preventing one from refining one's *middos.* This, too, may delude a person to think that he is fully observant of Torah, whereas in fact he is derelict in the very essence of Torah, "to cleave unto G-d" by emulating the Divine *middos.*

Let us take a look at the nature of a person's character traits, and what Torah expects of their refinement.

Anger

I elected to begin with the trait of anger because the Ramban, in his letter of guidance to his son, begins with instruction to control rage. Furthermore, the Arizal says that not only is rage a most decadent trait, but it is also distinct from other negative traits in that commitment of any sin causes a defect in a corresponding part of the body, whereas *rage corrupts the entire person* (cited in *Lev Eliyahu* vol. 3 p.21).

In keeping with the reason for this book, which is to assist in the struggle with the *yetzer hara* as it manifests itself in modern times, one may ask why the teachings of the earlier ethicists are not sufficient. The answer is that the escalation of angry behavior and its broad impact is unprecedented in the history of humanity.

Since the days of Cain and Abel, there has been hatred and strife. The first homicide was the result of Cain's rage at being slighted. World history is replete with wars and violence. However, the extent to which anger has soared and the degree to which we are exposed to it has never before occurred.

Hardly a week goes by in which there is not a report of an

incident of explosive anger. A disgruntled worker kills people at his former place of employment. A youngster shoots teachers and fellow students. Acts of terrorism are a daily phenomenon. Furthermore, these are delivered in the utmost explicitness via the graphic media. Awareness of these behaviors can arouse and intensify the inborn trait of anger. Repeated research studies have concluded that exposure to violence on television stimulates youngsters to violent behavior.

Let us not think that the horror which these acts elicit and their condemnation in any way minimize and discourage anger. To the contrary, the Torah tells us that the opposite is true. The Talmud says that one who has observed the humiliation of a suspected adulteress should avoid the use of wine, because alcohol lessens an individual's inhibitions and diminishes one's resistance to wrongdoing.

But should not the humiliation resulting from a sin serve to deter a person from wrongdoing and actually reinforce his resistance to sin? The answer is, No. Awareness of the grave consequences of sin does *not* diminish one's drive. The awareness that the sin was committed may actually *intensify* the drive, the punishment notwithstanding.

The wisdom of the Torah was borne out by recent studies. In the hope of discouraging young people from using drugs, some schools instituted a prevention program which consisted of lectures to students about the grave consequences of drug use. But, lo and behold! Research showed that those schools that had this "prevention" program had a greater incidence of drug use than comparable schools which did not have this program. Why? Because the youngsters were stimulated by hearing about the "highs" that drugs produced. The consequences of death or imprisonment incident to drug use was not a deterrent.

The pervasiveness of violence in today's world necessitates additional strategies to manage and control anger.

I have pointed out in other books that the Hebrew word for anger, *kaas*, is used for three different phases of anger, and this may lead to some confusion.

Kaas may refer to the feeling one has when one is offended or provoked. There is no need to describe this feeling. Everyone is familiar with it.

After we feel anger, we may react by expressing our anger in a wide variety of ways, from word to deed. In fact, clamming up and pouting is also a reaction, albeit a passive one. The *reaction* to the initial feeling of anger is also termed *kaas*.

The third phase of anger, which is likewise called *kaas,* is retention of the feeling. Sometimes the anger feeling dissipates, and at other times it may linger for hours, weeks and even years. We may hold a grudge for years against the person who offended us.

The reason that it is important to distinguish among these three phases is because the *feeling* one has when provoked is a reflex action, and it is not under voluntary control. Just as one does not have control whether or not to feel pain when pricked by a sharp instrument, neither does one have control whether or not to *feel* anger when one is offended. Inasmuch as this feeling is not under voluntary control, a person cannot be held culpable for this initial *feeling* of anger.

We do have control over how we react and how long we retain the feeling of anger. Since these phases are controllable, we are held responsible for them.

Yet, because *kaas* is used to describe all three phases, it may be assumed that it is wrong to *feel* anger when one is provoked. This is an error.

Proof of this is that Rambam writes that "having *kaas* is as grave a sin as idolatry" (*Hil. Dei'os* 2). Inasmuch as Rambam bases his rulings on the Talmud, there must be a source for this in Talmud. The Talmudic statement is, "*One who tears his clothes or breaks things in* **kaas** is equivalent to an idolater" (*Shabbos* 105b). It is clear that this is the source for Rambam's ruling, and that his use of *kaas* refers to the reaction to anger rather than to the initial feeling.

Finally, there is the retention of anger, or holding a grudge. This, too, is under voluntary control. It is of this that Solomon writes, "*kaas rests* in the bosom of fools" (*Ecclesiastes* 7:9). If one retains the feeling of anger instead of divesting oneself of it, one is indeed foolish.

To avoid confusion, I will use different terms for the various phases of anger. For the initial feeling upon being provoked, I will use the word "anger." For the reaction to this feeling and the expression of it, whether mild or severe, active or passive, I will use the word "rage." And for the grudge or retention of the feeling, I will use the word "resentment." I will ask the reader to pay attention to the specificity of these terms, in order to avoid any misunderstanding

The Torah forbids taking any kind of revenge, active or passive. It is forbidden to retaliate even verbally. If someone who has offended you asks for a favor, it is not permissible to say, "All right, I will do it for you even though you don't deserve it." Rather, you must do the favor and remain silent (*Leviticus* 19:18, *Rashi*).

A person may say, "I can restrain myself from taking revenge, and I can even restrain myself from telling someone he does not deserve it. But how do you expect me to not *feel* resentment? My feelings are not under my voluntary control."

If it would not be possible to overcome resentments, the Torah would not ask it of us. The Torah does not demand of us to do the impossible.

Inasmuch as any expression of a grudge is forbidden, there is simply no purpose in holding on to it. The only one who is harmed by a grudge is *the one who holds it*, not the one against whom it is held. Carrying a grudge may result in a variety of serious psychosomatic conditions, such as migraine headaches, high blood pressure and digestive disorders. It is certainly most foolish, as Solomon said, to do harm to yourself because of another person's behavior.

An excellent story that demonstrates Solomon's designation of one who harbors resentments as a fool is that of Graf Valentin Pototcki, the Righteous Convert of Vilna.

> Graf Pototcki was the son of a high nobleman, and his conversion to Judaism was a threat to the Church, which condemned him to death if he did not recant. Pototcki fled and lived incognito in a small village, where he spent his time studying Torah. The villagers knew his secret but, of course, would not expose him.
>
> There was a young boy in the village who often harassed him, and Pototcki pleaded with him to desist. The boy told his father that Pototcki had shouted at him and, to retaliate, the father revealed Pototcki's whereabouts to the Church. Pototcki was taken into custody and was told that if he did not retract his conversion, he would be burned at the stake.
>
> Pototcki refused to deny his faith and the cruel execution was carried out, with Pototcki's reciting the Shema with his last breath.
>
> The executioner, seeing that Pototcki was unperturbed by his imminent death, said, "You are no doubt thinking that when you get up to heaven you will bring down the wrath of G-d on us."
>
> "Not at all," Pototcki said. "When I was a child, I had little clay soldiers with which I played. One young boy was jealous of me and broke my soldiers. I cried to my father and asked him to punish the boy. When my father ignored me, I thought, 'Wait until I grow up and become the local feudal lord. I will then punish this boy.'
>
> "When I grew up and did have the power to punish him, I was mature enough to realize how foolish it was to make an issue of something as insignificant as a few

little clay soldiers, and I did nothing to punish the man who had broken them when he was a child.

"When I get to heaven and realize how insignificant is this puny little body that you are about to destroy, do you think I will make an issue of it?"

That was true wisdom. If we had the wisdom to think how insignificant the incident that angered us really was, we would not retain the resentment.

There are many anecdotes of how our Torah personalities overcame their feelings of resentment. One of them demonstrates not only their divesting themselves of resentment, but also the incomparable level of honesty they possessed.

A man came to R' Eliyahu Lopian asking his forgiveness for having offended him. "I don't recall you ever having offended me. How can I forgive something of which I am not aware?"

After some urging, the man told R' Lopian just how he had offended him. R' Lopian said, "It is easy for me to say that I forgive you, but I am afraid that this would just be lip service, and that in my heart I might still bear a grudge. My statement, 'I forgive you,' would be less than truthful.

"Please come back in two weeks," R' Lopian said. "In the interval, I will study the mussar writings on how to overcome resentments, so that my forgiving will be wholehearted."

Two weeks later the man returned. R' Lopian embraced him. "I forgive you with all my heart," he said, "and I want to thank you for giving me the opportunity to improve this important character trait."

The Arizal said, "Of all the methods of doing *teshuvah*, the most effective is to withstand offenses and insults and not react to them." R' Elazar Azcari said, "Why suffer in this world or in Gehinnom for your sins? You can dispense with the punishments by refraining from reacting when someone insults or humiliates you" (End of *Sefer Chareidim*).

> *The great merit of forgiving is demonstrated by an incident related by R' Chaim Shmulevitz. "During the Six Day War, we were assembled in a shelter, and we could hear the shells exploding around us. People were saying Tehillim (Psalms) fervently.*
>
> *"Then I heard an exclamation from a woman whose husband had abused her, and who had abandoned her for ten years, with no support for the children, all the while ada-mantly refusing to give her a get (Jewish divorce) to set her free. The woman said, 'Master of the universe! I forgive my husband for all the pain and agony he has caused me. Just as I have forgiven him, I plead with You to forgive the sins of all who are gathered here.' "*
>
> *R' Chaim said, "That our lives were spared was in the merit of this woman, who overcame the resentments she harbored against her husband who had so grieved her."*

Along with the mitzvah of restraining oneself from taking revenge and of not bearing a grudge is the mitzvah not to carry hatred in one's heart. We may sometimes dislike a person for his behavior because we do not know why he is acting that way. Perhaps if we knew all the facts, we would recognize that his actions were indeed proper. This is the principle of "Judge every person favorably" (*Ethics of the Fathers* 1:6). This is a derivative of the mitzvah to love your fellow as yourself. Just as you would want to be judged favorably and be given the benefit of the doubt, that is how you should act toward others.

R' Avraham Pam writes, "These days, given the stresses and tension of modern life, many people are irritable and depressed. This may cause them to say things they really do not mean, and they regret having said them. We should keep this in mind and give people every consideration" (*Atareh LaMelech* p. 84).

> *R' Aryeh Levin relates that he was attending a funeral in Jerusalem, and was surprised to see the deceased person's best friend leave the procession early and not accompany his friend to his final resting place. The friend eventually returned, having stopped off to buy a flower pot. "I was incensed," R' Levin said. "Why did he leave his friend's funeral to buy a flowerpot? Couldn't he have done it some other time? I did not want to transgress the Torah commandment, 'Do not carry hatred in your heart . . . reprove your fellow' (Leviticus 19:17), so I said to the person, 'Why did you leave the funeral to buy a flowerpot?'*
>
> *"The man replied, 'My friend died of a contagious disease, and the doctors ordered that everything he had come in contact with must be burned. Among his belongings were his tefillin. I pleaded with the doctors not to burn them, and they told me that if the tefillin were buried, that would be satisfactory. I stopped off to buy a flowerpot into which we could put the tefillin so that they could be buried in an earthenware container as the halachah requires. My friend's tefillin will be buried near him.'*
>
> *"The anger I had felt toward this person changed to great admiration," R' Levin said. "I then took a vow that I would always judge other people favorably."*

It is easy to find fault with others. That is why it is so helpful to say the introductory prayer before the morning service, composed by R' Elimelech of Lizhensk, which reads, "May we see the good traits of others and not their defects." Not only is this a valuable prayer in itself, but it also produces the proper mind-set for prayer, as the Arizal instructed, to commit ourselves to the mitzvah of "Love your fellow as yourself" before praying the morning service.

Anger may occur, as in the following example, when we lack knowledge of all the facts.

> I was once driving behind several cars up the ramp of a parking garage. The lead car was moving very slowly, and the driver of the car in front of me was tooting his horn angrily. I was tempted to do likewise but refrained because increasing the noise level would accomplish nothing. Inasmuch as I was already late for an appointment, I could feel the anger building up in me for the driver of the lead car, whose slow pace was further delaying me.
>
> When the lead car pulled into a space, I was able to see the handicap symbol on the license plate. Understanding why it was proceeding slowly totally dissipated my anger.

Nothing in creation is in vain. The Midrash says that when King David wondered why G-d had created insects that are nothing other than annoying, G-d showed him that he owed his very life to two insects (*Alef-Beis d'Ben Sira*). If anger were only destructive, it would not have been created. There must be a constructive aspect for anger, albeit not for rage or resentment.

The Baal Shem Tov said that all feelings, even those that we may consider to be contemptible, can be constructive if they are properly channeled. Let us see how this applies to anger.

This may come as a surprise to you, but pure "anger" is not what you may think. We need to re-define it.

Anger is the body's response to some kind of provocation. Pure anger is *not* hostility, hate or aggression. Those are actually part of the *reaction* to anger. *Anger itself is the way the body prepares itself to deal with an affront.* It is a physiological process, in which there may be an increase in the heart rate, tensing of the muscles, increased output of adrenaline, and several other changes.

Anger does not necessarily have to result in hostile feelings. It can be channeled constructively, as we shall see.

The problem is that from early childhood on we allowed anger to develop into hostile or aggressive feelings, and the two have become so closely intertwined that we consider them as one.

A further problem is that our early experiences were such that our reaction to anger usually worked. Perhaps we got what we wanted from parents who appeased us for the sake of peace and quiet. If nothing else, our reaction certainly gained us the attention of our parents. As we grew, we found that expressing anger toward people other than our parents often resulted in getting what we wanted. In other words, our expression of anger was often rewarded in one way or another. When an action is rewarded, we tend to repeat it. In this way, the expression of anger, which I have referred to as "rage," became one of our character traits.

Let me state at this point that the notion that "letting off steam" as a good way to get rid of anger is erroneous. This method of discharging anger is more likely to aggravate the body's response. Contrary to popular opinion, it does *not* get rid of the anger.

This was stated by the Talmud two thousand years ago. "Rage produces nothing but rage" (*Kiddushin* 41a).

Inasmuch as improper management of anger does not lessen it, the anger (= body response) may linger on. Instead of returning to normal, the body is likely to maintain its state of preparedness. Even if they are of lesser intensity, many of the physiological changes may persist. This is why improperly managed anger has been found to be associated with an increased incidence of heart disease, high blood pressure, stomach and intestinal disorders, migraine headaches and various muscular aches

Listen to what the Gaon of Vilna has to say about rage. "The anger response is based on one's assumption that fulfilling his desires is the ultimate good, the prime imperative of the universe. Within every angry person's mind lies the illusion, created by his pride, that everything and everyone surrounding him were created to serve his needs ... Because anger (=rage) is the ultimate expression of pride, anger and a feeling of closeness to G-d are mutually exclusive. One cannot subordinate himself simultaneously to G-d and to his own idolized self ... Anyone who wants to achieve closeness to G-d must exercise the opposite of pride: humility and self-effacement" (*The Juggler and the King* p. 41).

Constructive management of anger is going to require an "unlearning." We must detach the body response from the reaction with which it has been closely associated for many years. This is not going to be an easy or rapid process. However, if we appreciate how destructive our reaction to anger may be, and that rage is so grave a trait that the Talmud equates it with idolatry, we should be ready to undertake this difficult task.

Refining our character traits is a most essential if not *the* most essential component of *avodas Hashem*. This is often translated as "serving G-d." However, the word *avodah* means "work," and work requires effort and expenditure of energy.

It is related that the mother of the Chassidic master, R' Zvi of Ziditchov, would touch her sons' clothing when they returned from shul. If they were not moist with perspiration, she would tell them that their *davening* had lacked proper *kavannah* (concentration). The Talmud refers to prayer as *avodah shebelev*, the *work* of the heart. If they did not sweat during prayer, they obviously had not been working at it.

How is it that people who are meticulously observant of Torah may nevertheless become enraged and have outbursts of shouting, sometimes using very insulting words and even becoming physical? Why are they not restrained by the gravity of rage, which the Talmud equates with idolatry? The consequences of rage are most noxious. The Talmud says that when a person is in rage, "all the forces of Hell control him." And, "If he is a wise man, he loses his wisdom; if he is a prophet, he loses his prophesy" (*Pesachim* 66b). Should this not deter one from rage?

I found the answer in people who are addicted to dangerous drugs. They may be fully aware that using a drug may have the most serious consequences and may even be fatal. Even highly intelligent people may not be deterred by this. The reason is that *they do not know how to resist the compulsion.* Willpower is singularly ineffective. In treating a drug addict you must show him *how* to resist the temptation. Scare techniques do not work.

This is equally true of expressing anger. We all know the tricks of counting to ten or other devices to forestall rage. Yet, we so often fail to use them. Something more is necessary.

I must again resort to the example of the drug addict. Lecturing and reprimanding is worthless. He must be taught how to resist the compulsion, and this is by no means an easy task. Furthermore, once this is accomplished, he must continue *indefinitely* to practice the behavior that discourages drug use. Laxity in doing so may result in relapse.

Even if one learns how to overcome rage reactions, the risk of relapse is high. It is necessary to diligently continue these techniques. Ramchal in the introduction to *The Path of the Just* (*Mesilas Yesharim*) makes the point that knowledge of *what* one must do is inadequate. Even knowledge of *how* one can do it is not enough. Ongoing practice of the techniques for proper *middos* is necessary.

I learned a simple technique from my father, whom I never saw express rage. He used to say, "The person who is provoking me doesn't understand that what he is doing is very foolish. He thinks he is wise and right. I feel sorry for him that he is a fool. Pity and rage do not go together. You cannot be angry at someone for whom you feel sorry."

In contrast to "count to ten" maneuvers, the work at managing anger must begin well ahead of the provocation. If you are familiar with some of my other books, you may say, "Oh, Oh! There he goes again. This is going to be another essay on self-esteem." And you will be 100 percent right.

It is simple common sense: The better your self-concept, the less sensitive you are to comments that may be insulting or critical. The more capable you feel, the less you feel threatened by acts against your security.

As I have repeatedly pointed out, self-esteem is not vanity. The statement by the Chazon Ish that I cited earlier makes it clear that self-confidence is not vanity. To the contrary, a self-confident person will be receptive to opinions that differ with his own or to criticism. A person with little self-confidence may feel threatened by these and is apt to be closed minded.

Effective anger-management requires self-esteem. Indeed, mastery of anger is a major undertaking. People with little self-esteem may give up, saying, "That's too much for me. I'm not capable of doing that." That is the *yetzer hara* at work, discouraging a person from attaining mastery over anger.

No challenge is overwhelming when one has Divine assistance. The Talmud states that G-d helps those people who work at observing Torah, which, as we have seen, includes refinement of *middos*. We need just begin and be willing to make the effort.

Think ahead in preparation for any possible provocation. "Do I want to be in control, or do I want to react reflexively?" Every intelligent person will want to be in control of himself.

But it is important that you actually *say* this to yourself. "I do not want to be a pawn in the hands of others. I do not want others to control me. If someone else can provoke me to rage, then that person is controlling me. I refuse to let that happen."

The reason it is necessary to think ahead is because once a provocation has occurred, the physiological anger reaction may compromise our judgment. When your heart rate is increased and your muscles are tense as if in readiness for battle, it may be difficult to think clearly.

So think ahead. If someone will provoke you, what would you want the outcome of your reaction to be? The short-term effect might be that you put the person in his place, but the long-term effect is that your relationship will undoubtedly suffer. Is that what you really want? Were there not times that you regretted how you had responded in anger? Do you really want to do something that you may subsequently regret?

Be honest with yourself on this next one. Do you perhaps gloat or get a kick out of telling someone off? "Boy, did I ever tell him where to get off!" Anything you enjoy can bias your judgment. But, should you really be enjoying rage? After all, rage is not a commendable trait. Rage should be something that you abhor rather than bask in. If you can develop a feeling that rage is repulsive, this may influence your reaction.

The contemporary ethicist, R' Shlomo Wolbe, in *Alei Shur* (vol.1, p.160) says that a person should keep a journal in which he records his actions and feelings of the day. This is an extremely important method for analyzing and improving all character traits and is very helpful in anger management.

After a provocation, write down what happened. How was I provoked? How did I respond? Just what about that incident caused me to become angry? What did I want to accomplish with my reaction? In retrospect, would there have been a better way to react? If this were to happen again, how should I react?

You may find it difficult to keep such a journal. Remember, *avodah* means work, and refinement of character traits is *avodas Hashem.* Needless to say, this journal should be kept in a very private place, because you must be frank and honest in recording all your feelings.

Once anger occurs, it may escalate. It is, therefore, important to catch it at the earliest moment you feel it coming on. If you have prepared yourself for managing anger properly, you should promptly think, "I must remember what I wrote." This will bring to mind what you had written about controlling anger, and will enable you to implement these desired responses.

There is a polar opposite to expressing rage, and that is to train yourself, or better yet, be trained not to *feel* anger. We call this "repression." It is not as healthy a maneuver as it may seem.

We have defined anger as the changes in body preparedness. These changes can be directed toward constructive action and this will result in proper discharge of anger. Not feeling anger at all does not discharge it. What happens is that the feelings that are repressed are buried in the subconscious mind where you have no access to them, but from which they can influence your thoughts, feelings and actions in an unhealthy way.

Inasmuch as "rage" is the way anger is expressed, there is a broad spectrum of rage reactions, from very mild to very severe. Rage does not necessarily require screaming or throwing things. Even a response in a soft voice is technically rage, albeit very mild.

A rage reaction need not even be active. A person can react to a provocation by a silence which can be deafening. The "silent treatment" is a form of rage.

Passive rage may be more difficult to deal with than active rage. A child or grown-up may react by refusing to do what one is told. A person who was angered by his boss may fail to carry out an assignment. A person may fail to get something done because he overslept or missed his flight by a few minutes. The latter passive reactions are not only very subtle, but may be the result of a subconscious reaction. The person may be totally unaware that his missing the flight was his way of getting back at the boss.

Finally, a person may be angry with oneself. How often are we angry with ourselves because we made a mistake? We may be much more harsh with ourselves than we would be with someone else, and we may punish ourselves for making a mistake.

How deeply you feel anger will depend on your own particular sensitivity, just as pressure on your body may not cause pain unless your skin has become very sensitive due to sunburn, in which case even a soft touch may evoke pain. It is important that you try to understand why you felt hurt by another person, and record that in your journal. You will find that if you build self-esteem, you will be far less sensitive. You will now develop a positive self-reinforcing cycle. Gaining mastery over anger enhances your self-esteem, which makes it easier to increase your mastery.

If you apply these techniques diligently and regularly, you will succeed in managing one of the most potentially toxic traits. But this takes both time and effort. Do not expect instantaneous results.

You may ask: If I succeed in rage management, how does the energy generated in rage dissipate? Also, how can anger be channeled to constructive use?

You will recall that anger is *preparedness.* If a country expects an attack or wishes to attack, it mobilizes its army. If peace is achieved, it demobilizes and things go back to normal. Similarly, once you decide not to react with rage and you do not repress the feeling, the preparedness changes dissipate and you go back to normal functioning.

Channeling the energy of anger constructively takes a bit more effort and incentive.

The Torah tells us that when the Patriarch Jacob was reunited with his beloved son, Joseph, for whom he had grieved for twenty-two years assuming him to be dead, they embraced. Joseph wept, but Jacob did not weep. Instead, he recited the *Shema*.

The commentaries explain that when Jacob felt the enormous surge of emotion upon seeing his beloved son alive, he thought, *An intense emotion of love such as this should be directed toward love of G-d.* He, therefore, recited the *Shema*.

We are not capable of Jacob's spirituality, but we might nevertheless try to use the anger *energy* (=physiological response) constructively. Having avoided a rage reaction, we can promptly turn to Torah study or to reciting a chapter of *Tehillim* (Psalms). Expending the energy in this way may give one unexpected clarity in Torah and profound *kavannah* in prayer.

Our great Torah personalities were geniuses in good *middos* as well as in Torah knowledge. The two go together. One of the reasons they achieved such broad and profound knowledge and understanding of Torah is precisely because they had refined their *middos*. They redirected their energies and invested them in Torah study.

Isn't there an easier way to do this? No. It is *avodah*. Looking for the easy way is a trait that we will deal with in a subsequent chapter.

As we have seen, refinement of *middos* is a prerequisite to Torah and mitzvos. How is this achieved?

The letter of Ramban points the way. He tells his son to avoid rage, because by doing so he will achieve humility, "which is the finest of all the *middos*."

The obvious question is: Inasmuch as humility is the finest of all *middos*, why not begin with humility? Why begin with control of rage which will lead to humility?

The answer is that Ramban had an understanding of human psychology. Humility is a *feeling*, and it is very difficult to alter a feeling. Rage is an *action*, which is much more amenable to control.

Once a person has achieved control over rage, he has taken an important step by refining a character trait. This greatly facilitates refinement of other traits.

If someone replaces a shabby lounge chair in the living room, the old sofa now conflicts with the new chair, so the sofa must be replaced. The old carpet is now incompatible with the new furniture, so it must go, then the drapes, the wallpaper, the lamps, etc. The living room is now completely revitalized, and it all began with one chair!

The same is true of *middos*. The refinement of one trait makes the others incompatible. If rage is brought under control and this is maintained, refinement of other *middos* will come about more easily. One will still have to learn *mussar* diligently, but beginning with an "action trait" will facilitate development of humility and other commendable traits.

Reading Ramban's letter to his son once a week as Ramban suggested and praying for Divine assistance in the effort to overcome rage and resentment will not only result in character refinement, but will also lift the heavy burden of rage and resentment, allowing one to use one's energies much more efficiently.

Diligence

The Hebrew word, *zerizus*, is a bit difficult to define. It may be thought of as diligence, as industriousness, or as zeal. It is perhaps best defined as the antonym of laziness and sloth.

Ramchal stresses the importance of *zerizus*, and King Solomon devotes a significant portion of *Proverbs* describing and denouncing sloth and laziness. Clearly, these negative attributes have been with humanity for a very long time.

Yet, it is doubtful whether we were ever before as vulnerable to laziness as today. Turning the faucet can provide one with copious amounts of water. In the days of Ramchal, every bit of water had to be fetched from a well. The press of a button on a thermostat has obviated the laborious building and fueling a fire for warmth. In my youth, my mother had to open a chicken, check and remove the viscera, then soak it and salt it to drain the blood. Most observant housewives today do not even know how to "kosher" a chicken. Everything is bought ready for the pot. My mother made gefilte fish by purchasing a fish, cleaning and cutting it, then grinding it with a hand-grinder. Today, if we do not buy ready-to-eat gefilte fish, the most we do is put the frozen preparation into a pot.

It is hardly necessary to enumerate the countless ways in which technology has eliminated the need for exertion. Why bother learning how to do difficult calculations when a computer can do it more accurately and much quicker? We have even been spared the exertion of readjusting the car seat and rearview mirrors. The push of a button does it electronically.

The fallout of this is that we may have come to expect that there must be an easy way to get anything done. True, we wish to achieve *avodas Hashem*, but why can it not be accomplished like any other *avodah*, by just pushing a button?

Let us remember that *avodah*, in its original sense, means *real* work. There is no electronic *avodas Hashem*. We may make some use of technology in *avodas Hashem*, as by using a CD-ROM of Torah literature to find a quote, a source, or responsa. This may save us time that we can apply to Torah study. But Torah study requires *yegiah,* strenuous work. If it were possible to learn Talmud by having a tape recorder lecturing while one was asleep, this would not be proper acquisition of Torah, even if some knowledge could be absorbed by this method. The Talmud says that if a person claims to have mastered Torah without exertion, do not believe him (*Megillah* 6b). But what if he can demonstrate that he has indeed gained much Torah knowledge without exertion? Then he has absorbed some material that may be identical with Torah content, but it is not Torah, just as fool's gold may be bright and shiny, but is worthless. True Torah requires exertion.

One cannot discuss diligence and the avoidance of laziness without referring to the excellent section on the subject in *The Path of the Just.* Ramchal points out that the natural state of an object is to remain at rest, and the natural state of man is also inertia. One must exert effort to overcome this natural inclination.

Any attempt to overcome inertia is likely to be met with resistance. The human psyche is particularly adept to fabricate excuses to justify maintaining an undisturbed state of rest. The more intelligent a person is, the more clever are his rationalizations. These are not necessarily excuses given to *other people* for one's inaction, but rather excuses given to *oneself*. In other words, we may delude ourselves and believe our own excuses.

There are many instances where we may act with great diligence. If we have an early-morning appointment at which we will collect a substantial sum of money, we are likely to arise at the first ring of the alarm clock. We may have no difficulty arising early for an event that is pleasurable or which will bring us reward. People will respond to the alarm clock's arousal for a flight to Disneyland much differently than for a date at traffic court.

If we have our priorities in proper order, we can overcome the resistance to diligence. If we truly believe that proper behavior and virtuous deeds are all important, then we will more readily hasten to do them. If we understand the importance of *tefillah* (prayer), we will overcome the desire to linger in bed and promptly arise to avoid being late for the *minyan* (communal prayer).

How diligent one is in performance of mitzvos and character refinement is contingent on how much one understands that these are vital to achieve the ultimate goal of one's existence. This is true not only of diligence in doing the mitzvah but also of how diligent one is in the *quality* of the performance. Even if one hastens to shul early in the morning but fails to concentrate on the prayers and allows one's mind to wander in contemplation of what one intends doing throughout the day, that is dereliction in diligence. We *can* muster the proper *kavannah* (concentration) for *tefillah* if we make the effort.

We need not deny ourselves the gifts of modern technology, but we must be careful that they do not unduly influence us. We may enjoy the conveniences of modern life, but we should not be deluded that the goal of life is to live as comfortably as possible.

There is no question that our traits are subject to such influences. A trip to Israel takes a bit over nine hours instead of the four weeks it took in my childhood. The announcement over the airport public-address system that the flight has been delayed three hours should hardly cause a ripple. What are three hours compared to four weeks? Should we not be grateful that we can get there in twelve hours instead of four weeks? Yet, if you are like me, you probably gripe at the imposition of having to spend three hours at the airport.

The power of inertia can be so great that it can even result in laxity in behavior that is vital to life! Most smokers know that their habit may ruin their health and even kill them, and they indeed wish to live and to avoid crippling illnesses. Nevertheless, they may not be willing to make the requisite effort to break the habit.

Another reason why one may lack in diligence is the fear of failure. If I am very anxious that I may fail in what I wish to do, I may be reluctant to do it. People seem to accept passive failure more easily than active failure. If I am afraid that I may be turned down at a job interview, I may engineer things, consciously or subconsciously, to avoid that interview. Of course, if I do not show up for the interview, I will not get the job, but that seems to be more acceptable to some people than being turned down.

Here, too, self-esteem is a crucial factor. Failure is never pleasant, but it need not be devastating. A person with good self-esteem is indeed disappointed if he is turned down, but he thinks, "Too bad. I'll just have to try elsewhere." The person with low self-esteem may feel, "I'll never succeed in being hired," and feels that being turned down is so crushing a blow to his fragile ego that he must avoid it at all costs, and he avoids this disaster by not applying.

Another important component of diligence is *organization*. Unless one has one's priorities in order, one's life and daily routine may be in a state of chaos. If we have innumerable things to do and have not prioritized them, we may run helter-skelter from one thing to another and never fully attend to some of the most important things.

Prioritizing requires just paper and pencil and a bit of time. Give serious thought to what are really the most important things in your life. If you write these down in proper order, you have a much better chance of utilizing your time and energy wisely.

> *A man once complained bitterly to R' Levi Yitzchok of Berditchev that his business was failing. He was completely absorbed with this and could not think of anything else. His life had come to a standstill.*
>
> *R' Levi Yitzchok said, "You cannot think of anything else? Come, let us go to the mikveh." The man assumed that R' Levi Yitzchok intended to enhance his prayers for him by purifying himself in the mikveh. Once they were in the mikveh, R' Levi Yitzchok submerged the man's head underwater, and the man struggled to break free. R' Levi Yitzchok then said, "What was in your mind when I held your head under water?" "I wanted to breathe," the man said. "Were you thinking about your business then?" "No," the man said, "I just wanted to be able to breathe." "Then there is something more important to you than your business, isn't there? You should think of all the other things that are actually more important than your business and direct proper attention to them. Then you will act more constructively, and a more positive attitude will help you in your business as well."*

If you make your list, you will probably list your spouse and children as being of the highest priority. Then ask yourself, "Am I as diligent in attending to this highest priority as I am to things of lesser importance? Do I spend an inordinate time with work at the expense of neglecting my family?"

Hopefully, you will place your relationship with G-d and Torah high on your list. Do you devote the time and energy to this that it deserves?

We are very easily distracted by many things. Unless we clarify what is really most important to us and devote appropriate time and energy to these, our diligence will suffer.

Neither our time nor our energies are infinite. If we squander them, we will expend them on things of lesser importance at the expense of things that truly matter. Diligence is the key to most constructive functioning.

Spirituality vs. Hedonism

Hedonistic philosophy is probably as old as humankind, and little wonder. The human body has many cravings, and gratifying them is pleasurable. The newborn infant has only these cravings. Nonphysical strivings come only with maturation.

However, the possibilities for embracing a hedonistic outlook on life were never as great as they are today. In the past, the many hardships people confronted were not conducive to hedonism. Even as recently as the beginning of the 20th century, the average life span in the western world was under 40. Infant mortality was high. Childhood diseases and infectious diseases, especially pneumonia and tuberculosis, devastated populations. Those who survived these diseases lived in fear of epidemics. It was hardly likely that one could think that man was created to live in pleasure.

Work conditions were deplorable, and while there was relief from cold, there was nothing one could do to escape torrid heat. Transportation was slow and often dangerous. Even when food was not scarce, preparation was rather laborious.

Modern life is radically different. The average life span is 80. Epidemics are virtually unheard of. Air-conditioning gives us comfort on the hottest days. Much work is accomplished by machines, often controlled electronically. One can jet to the remotest parts of the globe in hours. One need not make an effort to go to the theater. All the entertainment one could wish for can be found in one's living room. Ready-to-eat foods are readily available, and the modern kitchen has simplified cooking. Many of the hardships that discouraged a hedonistic attitude have been eliminated.

I can remember, as a child, that there were only two varieties of kosher wine: sweet Concord, or sugarless dry wine, primarily for diabetics. Today there are more than 120 varieties of kosher wine! There is hardly any nonkosher food that is not available in a kosher counterpart. The Passover diet was sparse, devoid of the abundant delicacies and prepared foods available today. When I was a child, kosher Chinese, Korean, Italian, Japanese and Mexican foods were not imaginable. Kosher pizza was unheard of.

The Steipler Gaon writes, "When I was a child, our food was sparse and simple. Fresh fruits were a delicacy, available only infrequently. Candy was a special treat, and we had it on rare occasions. New clothes were almost unheard of. For Passover we might have a "new" suit that was pre-owned. We did not expect much, and when we got something, we appreciated it.

"Today's children are raised with abundance. They cannot appreciate a fruit or candy. They take everything for granted as being their due. If they do not get what they want, they feel deprived. They are angry at their parents and at the world for not giving them what they feel they have coming."

The elimination of many of the hardships of life and the provision of many types of gustatory delights and other indulgences have made hedonism a very real possibility for even the most observant Jew. If the *yetzer hara* wishes to imbue people with a hedonistic attitude, its work has been enormously facilitated.

There is nothing wrong with partaking of worldly pleasures. The problem with hedonism is that it makes pleasure-seeking the *goal and purpose* of life. Such an attitude makes spiritual life an impossibility. Spirituality requires that a person see the fulfillment of the longings of the *neshamah* (soul) rather than the body as primary.

The Jerusalem Talmud (*Kiddushin* 4:12) states that on Judgment Day a person will have to answer for not enjoying the goodness he was given but of which he did not partake. But when we partake of the pleasures of the world we must first recite a *berachah*, expressing our sincere gratitude to G-d for making pleasurable things available to us. Characteristic of this is the *berachah* we are to recite when we see a fruit tree in blossom: "Blessed is G-d Who did not omit anything from His world in order to give pleasure to His creations." When we acknowledge the Divine gifts and express our appreciation and gratitude to G-d, we are being spiritual.

On the other hand, physical indulgence for the sheer pleasurable experience without a spiritual component actually gives one the status of a *rasha*.

R' Eliyahu Lopian says that the popular concept of a *rasha* is one who frankly violates Torah. "Not necessarily so," says R' Lopian. "A person may pray three times a day and may shout *Shema Yisroel* in decibels, but if he is physically indulgent, even in permissible things, and does not subjugate his pleasurable activities to G-d, he is a *rasha*." R' Lopian cites Rabbeinu Yonah as his source for this remarkable statement (*Lev Eliyahu* vol. 1 p. 114).

A hedonist rejects all pain and discomfort as being antithetical to life. Judaism sees virtue and merit even in suffering.

The Talmud tells us that there is much that we can learn about proper living habits by observing nature (*Eruvin* 100b).

Have you ever wondered how a lobster can grow? It is a soft animal, encased in a rigid, unyielding shell. The answer is that as the lobster grows, its shell begins to be confining and oppressive. When the intensity of this discomfort increases, the lobster retreats to the safety of an underwater rock formation, sheds its shell and produces a more spacious one. When its continued growth again makes the new shell too oppressive, the process is repeated until the lobster reaches its maximum growth.

The stimulus for the lobster's growth is *discomfort*. If lobsters had access to tranquilizers and pain-relieving medications, their too-small shell would eventually cause their death.

Alas! Mankind does have access to alcohol and a variety of nostrums that relieve discomfort. Instead of recognizing discomfort as a signal that one should grow, many people resort to the quick relief of chemicals or a variety of pastimes, and never develop their spiritual potential.

It is, therefore, necessary that we resist the seductive lure of pleasure and make a concerted effort at spirituality.

It is noteworthy that Ramchal begins his primer on spirituality, *The Path of the Just*, with the chapter "The Duties of a Person in the World." Without the basic assumption that man has a duty in life rather than being nothing more than a pleasure-seeking animal of higher intellect (the *homo sapiens* of science), there cannot be a quest for spirituality.

How do we counter the modern *yetzer hara* of hedonism? By following Ramchal's advice in his introduction and reviewing *The Path of the Just* regularly, as well as intensely studying other works of *mussar*. We should follow Ramban's advice in the letter to his son, that after studying any portion of Torah we should think how we can apply it in our lives. This is especially true of *mussar*. Simply reading and even understanding *mussar* is sterile. We must give much thought to how we can apply these teachings in our lives.

In addition to the writings of *mussar*, the biographies of our great Torah personalities provide models of what a spiritual life consists. Emulating the lives of *tzaddikim* is a sure way toward development of spirituality.

Finally, we should follow the instructions in *Ethics of the Fathers*, "Make for yourself a teacher" (1:6). The Gaon of Vilna took these words literally. Knowing that it was unlikely that anyone would rebuke him, he engaged someone to regularly give him reprimand. Clearly, there was no one in his generation who was qualified to reprimand him. The Gaon, therefore, had to *make* someone his teacher, even if that person was far inferior to him.

Most people do not have that problem. We really do not have to *make* someone into a teacher. There is no dearth of competent teachers. Rather, we just have to coerce ourselves to submit to spiritual guidance.

Vanity

Of all objectionable human traits, Torah considers vanity the most loathsome. The Divine spirit never abandons even a very sinful person: "I will dwell among them even in their defilement" (*Leviticus* 16:16). Vanity, however, repels the Divine presence. "The abomination of G-d are those who are proud of heart" (*Proverbs* 16:5). G-d says, "A vain person and I cannot dwell in the same abode" (*Sotah* 5a). One of the chassidic masters interpreted the verse, "I stood between G-d and you" (*Deuteronomy* 5:5) as "the 'I,' or the ego, is what stands as a barrier between man and G-d."

The author of *The Ways of the Righteous* (*Orchos Tzaddikim*) states that the first stratagem of the *yetzer hara* is to cause a person to become vain. The Talmud says that without the help of G-d, a person could not possibly withstand the temptations of the *yetzer hara*. Inasmuch as the vain person rejects the Divine presence, he is at the mercy of the *yetzer hara*, which can then incite him to commit a variety of sins.

Rabbeinu Yonah makes a profound psychological observation. "*Vanity is an effort whereby a person tries to overcome a feeling of worthlessness"* (*Perush R' Yonah al HaTorah* p. 156). In my writings on self-esteem I have referred to Rabbeinu Yonah as a pioneer in elucidating the toxic effects of low self-esteem.

Rabbeinu Yonah's observation is of great importance in understanding a common psychological disorder. There are people who are always demanding to be served, honored and obeyed. They are inconsiderate and often intolerant of others, and may be domineering and abusive. Psychotherapy is not very successful in treating this condition.

In psychological texts this personality disorder is termed "narcissism." The name is derived from a myth about Narcissus, a very handsome man who fell in love with himself when he saw his reflection in the water. Hence, a person who loves himself is said to be "narcissistic."

Rabbeinu Yonah's comment explains that the narcissistic person's insatiable demands give the appearance that he loves himself, and that he feels the world revolves around him. Actually, he is a person who thinks so little of himself that he despises who he is. His incessant demands to be loved and honored are a psychological defense. The attention he receives gives him a feeling that he is not unworthy. However, this feeling is very transient. His feelings of being unlovable, unlikable and unworthy resurface, leading to further demands for ego gratification.

The myth of Narcissus has an interesting counterpart in Talmud. A Nazirite brought his offerings to the Temple at the completion of his vow. This ritual requires that the Nazirite shave his hair. Inasmuch as he had beautiful flowing locks, the High Priest, Shimon HaTzaddik, asked him why he had taken a vow which would necessitate shaving his beautiful hair.

The young man replied, "One time, I went to fetch water and I saw my handsome image in the water. The *yetzer hara* overtook me and wished to destroy me with self-infatuation. I said to myself, "Why are you vain in a world that is not yours, in which you will ultimately be lowered in a grave to be fed upon by worms? I then made a vow to become a Nazirite, and shave my beautiful hair as a service to G-d" (*Nedarim* 9b).

In this story, the young man also admired his handsome features, but he quickly realized that a spurious self-love would be destructive. He had a healthy self-esteem which enabled him to realize that superficial appearances are meaningless. He knew that he had a purpose in existence, that physical life comes to an end and that true life consists of a relationship to G-d. This is truly caring for oneself, and is a healthy self-love.

The need for a healthy self-love is indicated by the Torah commandment "Love your fellow as you do yourself" (*Leviticus* 19:18). Some commentaries ask: Why does the Torah advocate self-love as the basis for interpersonal relationships? The answer is that the Torah is referring to true self-love, which is the love for one's Divine *neshamah* (soul), which is the real "self" rather than the physical body which disintegrates after its brief sojourn on earth. Spurious self-love, that of the narcissist, makes it impossible for a person to love or to be considerate of others.

We are composed of two components, body and soul. The vital force within animals is not the same as the *neshamah* of man. In creation of man, "G-d blew into his nostrils the soul of life" (*Genesis* 2:7). The Zohar points out that when one exhales, one breathes out from within oneself. Therefore, when G-d blew the soul of life into man, it was a G-dly soul, of G-d Himself.

Inasmuch as G-d is absolute unity, all *neshamos*, by virtue of their G-dliness are also a unity. That we are separate beings is because we have physical bodies that have boundaries. To the extent that we emphasize the *neshamah*, to that extent we are one. To the extent that we emphasize the physical body, to that extent we are separate.

A person who truly loves his *neshamah* also loves the *neshamos* of others. This is a love of the real self, the *neshamah*, which is not narcissistic. It is when we seek the gratification of our physical desires, when one favors the body above the soul, that one has a spurious self-love, since the body is but a receptacle for the real self. This spurious self-love is what is referred to as narcissistic.

In *Life's Too Short* I describe a variety of psychological defenses and behavioral tactics whereby a person may try to escape the intense discomfort of feeling incompetent and inadequate, feelings which are invariably not justified by fact. Paradoxically, the most intense feelings of low self-esteem are particularly likely to occur in gifted people. Some people develop grandiose feelings to avoid the pain of feelings of little worth. I elaborated on the subject of self-esteem in *Angels Don't Leave Footprints.*

We do not know whether low self-esteem was as prevalent in earlier times as it is today. If it is indeed more common today than in the past, there are a number of factors that may be responsible for this.

Life in the *shtetl* (village) and even in larger towns was very different from modern urban life. Many generations lived in the same community, and a person had an identity of belonging to a family. Many people were identified by their lineage rather than by surnames. My father used to speak of "Baruch Yochanan's" (Baruch, the son of Yochanan). He did not know his last name. Sometimes the identification went another generation farther; e.g., "Feivel Moshe Pessy's *dem chazzan's*" ("Feivel Moshe, son of Pessy, who was the daughter of the cantor"). The current interest in tracing one's roots indicates the importance people ascribe to their genealogy. People who were identified by their ancestry gained a measure of self-esteem.

This is much different than modern living, where not only is there no continuity of lineage within a community, but any one individual may live in various cities as his company may transfer him to where they need him or as employment opportunities change. This may prove especially traumatic for children, who have to undergo the adjustment of being "the new kid on the block" numerous times.

The concept of "mass production" characterizes not only industry, but people as well. Our educational institutions "mass produce" students. They emerge as if all were cast in one mold. There is rarely any individuality in thought. This is further aggravated by the mass media, which control what people think by dispensing selected information. There can hardly be much self-esteem when there is no real "self."

In the days of yore, there were teacher-student relationships. A student's self-esteem was enhanced when an instructor took a personal interest in him. This relationship has been grossly diluted.

Seeing oneself as a mere fragment of the mass of humanity does little for one's self-esteem. In a modern city, thousands upon thousands are lined up on the highways. Throngs of people dart to and fro much like ants at an ant colony, and hordes of humanity are pushed like so many sardines into subway cars. Such scenes do not allow one to feel very significant.

Years ago, people thought that the earth was the center of the universe and that everything revolved around it. If our planet was so significant, then its inhabitants might have some significance. Modern science has given us an awareness of the vastness of the known universe. There are billions of stars, some of which are billions of light-years away. (A light-year is 5.88 trillion miles.) On a celestial map, the sun is but a third-rate star, and the planet Earth would not even show up as a speck. "How then," says the *yetzer hara*, "do you have the chutzpah to think of yourself as significant?"

Utilizing this tactic, not only does the *yetzer hara* cause a person to have a carefree attitude, but also makes him feel that he is a totally insignificant creature. As Rabbeinu Yonah says, this feeling of nothingness is intolerable, and a person may react to this with a feeling of grandiosity.

The chapter on "Vanity" in *Orchos Tzaddikim* is "must" reading. The author wisely points out that even vanity does not eliminate the misery of feeling insignificant. A person may, therefore, seek other ways of escaping this discomfort, and this may lead to a variety of indulgences. "Vanity leads to lust, for the vain person's heart is expansive and desires everything."

The first technique to thwart the wile of the *yetzer hara* is, therefore, to develop a healthy self-esteem, which goes hand in hand with true humility. G-d chose Sinai, the lowest of the mountain range, as the site for giving the Torah because He loves those who feel humble. Yet, He did not give the Torah in a valley because He does not want us to feel so low that we are crushed by feeling insignificant. G-d has designated us as His children, and made His love for us known to us by calling us His children (*Ethics of the Fathers* 3:18). We are privileged to be princes in the royal court. But rather than considering that our status makes us superior to others, we should realize that it imposes upon us the awesome responsibility of avoiding doing things that are beneath our dignity.

A person can achieve greatness without becoming vain. We are fortunate in having people who personally witnessed the Chafetz Chaim, a person who knew that his encyclopedic knowledge of Torah justified him in becoming virtually the final authority in halachah, yet whose humility is legendary. It is of great *tzaddikim* such as this that G-d says to the angels, "Look at the masterful creature that I created" (*Bereishis Rabbah* 12).

I was delighted to find my concepts of self-esteem and vanity confirmed by the great Torah scholar of our generation, R' Aharon Kotler. At the risk of redundancy, I wish to cite his essay in *Mishnas R' Aharon* vol. 1 pp. 157-159:

'You are children unto G-d — you shall not cut yourselves and you shall not make a bald spot between your eyes for the dead" (Deuteronomy 14:1). Rashi comments, 'Because you are the children of G-d, it is fitting that you be attractive and becoming.' In other words, over and above that this is a measure of respect toward G-d, it is also because of your own great worth.

In the subsequent verse, the Torah continues, "For you are a holy nation . . . and G-d chose you to be unto Him a treassured people." This is how far the level of each Jew reaches: Children unto G-d — Beloved is man, who was created in the image of G-d; Beloved is Israel, who are called Children unto G-d — a holy nation and a treasured nation.

As a general rule, a person does not recognize his awesome importance, and recognizes in himself only his lowliness, for this is familiar to him due to his physicality and his habits since infancy — 'Man is born a wild foal' (Job 11:12) — 'For the nature of a person's heart is evil from his youth (Genesis 8:21).' Consequently, he sees himself as worthless and shameful, and as a result of this (self-perception) he indeed does become progressively more stunted. This is analogous to a wealthy person who is unaware of his wealth, and consequently cannot use it, which results in his living as if he were poor.

A person should be aware of and reflect on the great worth that is within him and on the power that actually develops from the recognition of this worth. The greater the recognition of this, the more his worth increases. This is a major and principle factor in the rectification of one's actions, because knowing his worth, one will always reflect whether a given act is fitting and proper for him and will refrain from any act or conduct that is beneath his dignity, because 'as Children of G-d you should be becoming.'

All the more so one who studies the Divine Torah, which gives him a status similar to kohanim (priests) for whom the above restrictions are more stringent. There is also the mitzvah 'You shall be holy,' for the greater one's holiness in the service of G-d and in bringing His offerings, the more stringent is this mitzvah. Certainly a Torah scholar who is constantly engaged in Torah study and is the darling child of G-d, how much more must be becoming and be cautious not to behave indecently (especially because people observe him and scrutinize his conduct, and it is their nature to look for defects in anyone who is superior to them. This places a great responsibility on him that his conduct be becoming and free of anything indecent and dishonorable).

Now when the Torah says, 'The Holy One is in your midst,' and the Talmud explains this as meaning that the Holy One is within each person, this must be taken literally. How, then, can one do anything that offends the Holy One within him or banish Him from one's midst? If we reflect on this, we are seized with awe and trembling ... The greatest cause of sin is that a person does not feel worthy (being unaware that there is G-dliness within him). This is why we have said that awareness of one's worth is a major factor in rectification of one's behavior ...

It is obvious that concepts such as these and reflecting upon them will not in any way result in vanity. To the contrary, he will have a feeling of humility, because the more spiritual a person is and the more he approaches holiness the more he effaces himself ... True concepts are the core of humility, and the more removed one is from truth, the more vain one becomes. One will greatly inflate any positive trait one finds within oneself, whether a physical characteristic (since one removed from truth emphasizes the physical), and even more so a spiritual characteristic. But if one is aware that the Holy One is within him and that he is a child unto G-d, he is in a state of growth and is constantly aware of how much he is still lacking, and that there are no grounds for considering himself to have achieved so much."

I hope that the words of this great sage will once and for all do away with the objection that to have self-esteem is to be vain. As Rabbi Kotler so clearly points out, knowing that there is G-dliness within oneself should result in a feeling of dignity and the awareness of one's potential. By the same token, one should be exceedingly humble in realizing how little of one's potential to achieve spirituality one has actually exercised.

The depressing feeling of nothingness, of being lost in the mass of humanity in a bustling metropolis, can be offset if a person realizes, "G-d is within me. He created me for a specific purpose. If my assignment could be fulfilled by any other person or even by all these millions of people together, then my existence would be superfluous. I am not just another ant in an ant colony. I am unique, with a unique mission for which I was created, and I have the ability to fulfill that mission."

Of course, this presumes that a person believes that he was specially created. This belief, too, is subject to a modern-day challenge which we shall next examine.

Belief

The basis of Judaism is belief in G-d, the G-d of Abraham, Isaac and Jacob. The *yetzer hara* is especially focused on undermining belief.

Belief in G-d has been an issue of struggle throughout our history because Jews are by nature skeptical. Other nations were credulous, easily accepting anything as a god. The behavior of the Israelites, as reported in the Torah, indicates that in spite of the most amazing miracles G-d performed for them, they continued to doubt Him.

The Midrash states that before offering the Torah to the Israelites, G-d offered it to the nations of Edom, Ishmael and Moab, so that they should not complain that they were denied it. When they asked what Torah observance required of them, G-d said to Edom, "You shall not kill"; to Ishmael, "You shall not steal"; and to Moab, " You shall not commit adultery." These nations rejected the Torah as making impossible demands of them.

R' Yitzchok Meir of Gur asked, "How did this forestall their complaining? When G-d gave the Torah to the Jews He began with, 'I am the Lord your G-d.' Perhaps had He said this to the other nations, they would not have rejected it."

R' Yitzchok Meir answered, "The function of Torah is to help a person master his strongest innate immoral drives. That of Edom was murder, that of Ishmael was theft and that of Moab was lust. They were, therefore, challenged with these commandments. None of these are the primary weaknesses of Jews. The Jewish Achilles' heel is skepticism. Jews can be obstinate when it comes to belief. They were, therefore, challenged with accepting 'I am the Lord your G-d.' "

However, throughout the ages, Jews developed an intense belief in G-d, repeatedly accepting martyrdom rather than surrender their faith.

But the *yetzer hara* has not given up. It constantly seeks ways to undermine our belief in G-d.

In the latter half of the 20th century, the *yetzer hara* acquired a new weapon. As a result of unprecedented scientific, medical and technological advances, much of mankind came to believe that the human genius could find the answer to everything. All of mankind's misery could be eliminated, and science would produce a Paradise on earth. Man's reason was enthroned as being superior to every-thing. There was no longer any need for G-d. In the 60's, "G-d is dead" became the motif of young people. This ushered in an epidemic of drug use, whereby morality fell by the wayside, and thousands of young people lost their lives in pursuit of the ephemeral pleasure produced by chemicals.

The Talmud makes an interesting comment. Referring to the repeated relapses of the Israelites into idolatry, the Talmud states that the Jews were not so foolish as to believe that the idols were gods. Rather, because they wanted to be free of the restrictions imposed by God and the Torah, they sought to supplant the Torah with a god they could control (*Sanhedrin* 63a).

"Free of restrictions" is the calling card of the *yetzer hara.* This is the antithesis of Judaism.

The greatest achievement in Judaism was attained by Moses, who earned the unique appellation of *eved Hashem,* a servant of G-d. The aim of the Jew is expressed in the *Shema,* which is the expression of acceptance of the sovereignty of G-d. It is our goal to acknowledge G-d as our master and to be His obedient servants.

In an interesting discussion, the Talmud concludes that a person who performs the mitzvos as mandatory is more deserving than one who does so of his own free will. Why? Because the former must overcome the inherent human resistance to obeying an order, whereas one who performs mitzvos of his own free will does not have this struggle. It is precisely doing battle with the *yetzer hara* that is most meritorious (*Kiddushin* 31a).

It is related that a chassid complained tearfully to R' Menachem Mendel of Lubavitch (*Tzemach Tzedek*), "Woe is me! What can I do? I have no desire to study Torah." R' Menachem Mendel's eyes welled up with tears. "Woe is me!" he said. "What can I do? I *do* have a desire to study Torah." R' Menachem Mendel felt that studying Torah because he loves to do so is not the complete mitzvah. Doing a mitzvah means obeying a command, not doing something because it is pleasant.

The Talmud (*Sanhedrin* 91b) cites a dispute between R' Yehudah HaNasi and the Roman satrap, Antoninus. R' Yehudah held that the *yetzer hara* enters a person at the moment of conception. Antoninus argued that if this were so, the fetus would kick his way out of the womb, and R' Yehudah conceded.

R' Avraham Grodzinsky asks: Why would the *yetzer hara* wish to leave the womb to a certain death? What pursuit of pleasure can a fetus possibly have? He answers that the primary drive of the *yetzer hara* is not so much the pursuit of pleasure as *the desire to throw off all restrictions.* If the fetus had a *yetzer hara,* it would go to its death in the desire to escape the confinement of the womb.

The skepticism which R' Yitzchok Meir cited as being characteristic of Jews can be understood in this light. Jews do not have a genuine philosophical doubt of G-d. Rather, their skepticism is one of convenience. They do not wish to be restricted. Denying G-d permits them to gratify the drives forbidden by the Torah. All philosophical arguments against belief in G-d are simply rationalizations, which is defined as "giving good reasons instead of true reasons." It is beneath their dignity to admit that they wish to be free to gratify all their drives. It is much more respectable to claim that they do not believe in G-d because they have come to this conclusion purely on an intellectual basis.

King David stated this succinctly. "The degraded person says, 'There is no G-d' " (*Psalms* 14:1). R' Samson Raphael Hirsch explains that "the degraded person" is someone who is completely dominated by his physical cravings. It is this person who defensively denies the existence of G-d.

As we noted earlier, our era is one of unprecedented hedonism, which is the very antithesis of spirituality. It is only logical that the *yetzer hara* would seize this opportunity to undermine belief in G-d. The unprecedented pursuit of pleasure has made us more vulnerable to the *yetzer hara's* attack on faith.

King David cited the grandeur of the world as testimony to Divine creation (*Psalms, chs.* 19, 104). Rambam says that an appreciation of the marvels of the world will result in an intense love for G-d. Neither of them had access to the scientific instruments which have shown us the incredible design in both the macrocosm and microcosm.

Some scientists felt threatened by belief in G-d. Their narrow attitude was not only that what cannot be scientifically proven *may* not exist. Rather, their dogmatic assertion was that what cannot be proven *cannot* exist.

Anyone following the latest scientific discoveries realizes that many scientists have discarded earlier theories, and are accepting, if only reluctantly, that creation is the only logical explanation for the existence of the universe (*Permission to Believe*. Lawrence Keleman, Targum/Feldheim, 1990). Just as any fighter threatened with defeat strikes out in a desperate last effort, the *yetzer hara,* sensing that reasonable people will become believers, is vigorous in its effort to undermine Torah, and is exploiting hedonism to its advantage.

A person who thinks seriously will come to the realization of the truth of G-d.

When Moses first told the Israelites that G-d had appeared to him and that they would be emancipated, Pharaoh said, "Increase their workload so that they do not have time to listen to Moses" (*Exodus* 5:9). Today the *yetzer hara* utilizes a similar technique. "Keep people's minds occupied with other things. Fill every bit of their nonworking hours with insipid and titillating television sitcoms and other pastimes. Do not allow them to think." In this way, the *yetzer hara* tries to bar people from thinking seriously. If people who profess that they do not believe in G-d and in the Torah will be questioned carefully and will be truthful, they will admit, albeit reluctantly, that they have done more research on what stock to buy than on the existence of G-d.

This is a tactic of the *yetzer hara* of the 21st century.

The primary defense against the *yetzer hara* of skepticism is, therefore, to resolve that one will search for the truth, even if this will deprive him of being free to do whatever one wishes.

> *I wish to share with you an amusing anecdote. One patient at my rehabilitation center refused to attend the meetings of Alcoholics Anonymous. "They talk too much about G-d," he said. "I am an atheist, and G-d talk is not for me."*

One day, he appeared at a meeting. I could not restrain myself, and asked him, "What made you change your mind?"

The man replied, " I was sitting in my room, looking out the window at the beautiful trees. The thought occurred to me, 'Who is taking care of those trees? Whoever it is certainly is doing a better job than I have done with my life.' So I decided to come down."

The prophets sometimes compare sinful people to alcoholics. In absences of liquor, their behavior is nevertheless that of an intoxicated person. We may expand on the prophet's insight.

My clinical experience has shown that the basic defect in the alcoholic is the refusal to accept that he is not in control of every facet of his life, especially the use of alcohol. Even the most traumatic consequences cannot convince him otherwise. *The active alcoholic is his own god.* He cannot, therefore, accept that there is a Power superior to him.

Torah literature refers to *ol malchus Shamayim,* accepting the yoke of the sovereignty of G-d. Indeed, the sharpest epithet in Torah is *beliyaal* (= *bli ol,* without a yoke). The person who wishes to be free of all restrictions cannot submit to a higher authority. The person who denies G-d is, very much like the alcoholic, someone who wishes to be his own god.

A thinking person will realize, "I am mortal. Regardless of my strengths, I am not all powerful. There may indeed be a Being that is All powerful." The willingness to consider this possibility is the first step to overcome the denial of G-d.

A physician specializing in infertility said, "I was not a religious person. One day, I was peering through a microscope at a fertilized ovum. It occurred to me that from this point on, all that will be added to this ovum are nutrients, primarily carbon, hydrogen, nitrogen and oxygen, and from these elements this ovum will develop into a complete human being. The human body is an organism of incomparable complexity and efficiency. The liver is more efficient than a fully computerized factory seven stories high. The human brain with its more than fourteen billion cells which are all interconnected in an unfathomable network can produce the analytic thought of the Talmud and its commentaries as well as symphonies of Beethoven, the works of Shakespeare and the discoveries in physics of Newton and Einstein. This tiny, microscopic ovum will fashion this marvelous creature out of simple elements. It was then that I realized that there must be a G-d."

What enormous mental effort it must take to override the obvious and to deny G-d! The only explanation for arriving at so absurd a conclusion is that one's thinking has been grossly distorted by one's desire to be free of any and all restrictions.

We should have sufficient pride not to allow the unique capacity of the human intellect to be distorted by the desires that issue from the animalistic drives that issue from the physical component of our being.

Of course, our tradition is a foundation of our belief. It is related that prior to beginning the Seder, a man said, "We are going to conduct the Seder and relate the miracles of the exodus from Egypt the way my father did. He emulated his father, and so it has been handed down in an unbroken chain from generation to generation all the way back to the generation that experienced the exodus and saw the miracles with their own eyes. "

Just a bit of unbiased reflection will indicate that a tradition observed by millions of people and transmitted without interruption from generation to generation is not to be doubted.

Hashgachah Pratis (Divine Providence)

Our generation has been put to a stringent test of *emunah* (faith and trust in G-d). The unparalleled horror of the Holocaust and the terrorism in Israel has caused many people to ask, "Where is G-d? Why is He silent?"

From the time that G-d told the Patriarch Abraham, "Know with certainty that your offspring shall be aliens in a land not their own, they will enslave them and will oppress them four hundred years" (*Genesis* 15:13), and until this day, Jewish history has been pockmarked with disasters. The fall of Judea, the Inquisition, the Crusades, the blood libels, the pogroms, the Holocaust — all have put our faith to the test.

Questioning the silence of G-d is not new to Jews. Moses said, "My G-d, why have You done evil to this people . . . From the time I came to Pharaoh to speak in Your Name, he did evil to this people, but You did not rescue Your people" (*Exodus* 5:23). The Psalmist says, "Show that You are awake. Why do You wish to appear as if asleep?" (*Psalms* 44:24). "My G-d, my G-d, why have You forsaken me, and the words of my cry are far from my help? My G-d, I call by day but You do not answer, and at night, but there is no pacification for me" (*Psalms* 22:2-3).

The Talmud makes an amazing statement. Moses referred to G-d as "great, mighty and awesome" (*Deuteronomy* 10:17). The prophet Jeremiah said, "Heathens are dancing in His Sanctuary! Where is His awesomeness?" and he did not refer to G-d as awesome. Daniel said, "Heathens are enslaving His people! Where is His might?" and he did not refer to G-d as great. The Talmud asks: How did they dare digress from what Moses said? The Talmud answers that because they knew that G-d was absolute truth, they did not say what they did not perceive with their own eyes to be true. The Men of the Great Assembly said that, to the contrary, the might and the awesomeness of G-d is evident from the fact that this tiny nation has been driven from its homeland, persecuted and decimated, "a helpless lamb surrounded by seventy hungry (and hostile) wolves," and yet it survives (*Yoma* 69b).

Moses, indeed, asked G-d to let him understand the mystery of His ways (*Exodus* 33:13). The Talmud says that G-d told Moses that it was impossible for any living mortal to grasp this (*Berachos* 7a).

But Moses, the Psalmist, Jeremiah and Daniel's questioning did not weaken their faith and trust in G-d. Our unfaltering faith in G-d is evident from the fact that so many of the survivors of the Holocaust have remained staunchly devoted to G-d.

R' Yechezkel Abramsky said that the conditions of slave labor in Siberia were worse than death. When he awoke in the morning and said *Modeh Ani* (I thank You), he would think, *What do I have to look forward to today? Beatings and humiliation, that's all. I will not have a free moment to even think of Torah. For what am I saying Modeh Ani? But when I got to the words 'abundant is Your faithfulness; I felt strengthened and inspired. My captors can deprive me of studying Torah, and they can deprive me of doing mitzvos, but they cannot deprive me of my belief in G-d, and for that I am thankful.*

The Talmud says that Moses wrote the Book of Job, an account of terrible disasters that befell a G-d-fearing man. Job could not reconcile Divine Providence with the calamities he suffered, and concluded that G-d must have abandoned the world and left it to the insentient and relentless physical laws of nature. Three of Job's friends tried to convince him that his misfortunes were by Divine Providence, giving various explanations why G-d would have done this to him. Job rebutted all their arguments.

G-d then spoke to Job, "Where were you when I created the world?" In other words, only one who had a complete grasp of eternity and infinity could understand why any event occurred. Since no human being, wise as he may be, has so comprehensive a grasp, it is impossible for any human to understand why certain things occur.

Yes, many people have questioned G-d. The Chafetz Chaim said, "For one who believes, there are no questions. For one who does not believe, there are no answers."

Envy, Desire and Pursuit of Acclaim

"Envy, desire and the pursuit of acclaim take a person out of the world" (*Ethics of the Fathers* 4:28).

Envy is hardly a recent phenomenon. Cain's murder of Abel was the outcome of envy. The Ten Commandments explicitly forbid envy. Solomon says, "Envy is the rot of the bones" (*Proverbs* 14:30). Since man's appearance on earth, envy has been one of the character traits the *yetzer hara* has continuously exploited.

Envy is either foolish or of a criminal nature. If one intends to acquire the object he covets, then his intention is criminal. If he has no intention of acquiring it, then envy is nothing but a gnawing feeling of dissatisfaction, giving a person no peace of mind. As Solomon says "The envy of one person of another is futility" (*Ecclesiastes* 4:4). Yet, this destructive trait has plagued mankind throughout history and has ruined both individuals and nations.

Given the persistence of envy since antiquity, is there any reason to be more concerned about it today?

There have always been the wealthy, and there have always been the poor. No doubt, some of the poor have always envied the wealthy, and some of the less wealthy have envied the wealthier. Although envy has always existed, it is probably greater today both quantitatively and qualitatively.

It is said that the philosopher, Immanuel Kant, standing in front of a store window where many items were exhibited, said, "I never before knew that there were so many things I can do without." But in Kant's time there was no advertising industry, or certainly not one as sophisticated as today. Marketing is one of the most important components of commerce, with a psych-ology specialty all its own. Television and radio commercials as well as billboards, newspapers and magazines do not merely announce available wares, but cleverly convince the populace that if they do not have these items, they are being deprived of a pleasure which is legitimately theirs. The adver-tising industry has joined the *yetzer hara* in exploiting man's envy.

Whereas *tzenius* (modesty) is especially important in Torah living, there has always been a modicum of modesty in the secular world. The total abandonment of modesty today has resulted in provoking a feeling of dissatisfaction among some people, who are made to feel that whatever they have is inadequate.

It may be difficult to convince people who may lack means that there are really no grounds for envying the affluent. There is a Midrash about a bird that approached a well-fed bird in its cage. "How fortunate you are to have abundant food supplied to you every day. I must hunt for my food, and I often go hungry." The other bird replied, "You see only the food my master gives me, but you don't see the cage that imprisons me. I would readily trade my food for your freedom" (*Yalkut Shimoni, Koheles* 12).

It has been said that if everyone's life conditions were placed into bundles and people were given a choice, every-one would choose his own. My clinical experience has con-firmed the validity of this aphorism. Some of the people who have consulted me for the most agonizing suffering are precisely those people who are the object of people's envy. It may seem that to be a some'ach bechelko (satisfied with whatever one has) one must be highly spiritual. This is not necessarily so. One need only know the true circumstances of those people whom one considers to be more fortunate.

Whereas desire is always a component of envy, there can be desire without envy. A person may have many cravings for things that are not the possessions of others. Although such desire lacks the opprobrium of envy, it, too, can "take a person out of the world."

One of the reasons that envy, desire and the pursuit of acclaim can actually result in destroying a person is because they have no end point. An envious person is never satisfied. A person who lusts for things never has enough, as the Talmud says of this person, "A person does not die having satisfied even half of his cravings" (Koheles Rabbah 1:34), and a person who seeks to be honored never feels that he has been sufficiently appreciated.

> In the Yeshivah of Radin there was a scholar who sought recognition from the students. He would try to impress them with his sagacity, but instead of gaining their respect, he found that they avoided him.
>
> One day he approached the Chafetz Chaim and said, "You and I are both Torah scholars. Why is it that you are honored wherever you go, but I am not respected by anyone?"
>
> The Chafetz Chaim responded, "The Talmud says, 'Everyone who seeks acclaim, the acclaim will flee from him. Everyone who shuns acclaim, the acclaim will pursue him' (Eruvin 13b). Why does the Talmud stress 'everyone'?
>
> "What the Talmud means," the Chafetz Chaim continued, "is that even if a person is not learned or particularly pious, nevertheless, if he shuns acclaim, he will

receive it anyway. On the other hand, there is a person who is very accomplished and would be honored, but if he seeks and pursues acclaim, he will not get it.

"That is the difference between us," the Chafetz Chaim said. "Your Torah scholarship would indeed warrant that you be respected, but because you seek to be honored, you do not receive it. Acclaim flees from you. I, on the other hand, do not deserve to be honored. My Torah knowledge and deeds hardly warrant it. But by nature, I despise acclaim, and precisely because I shun it, it pursues me."

The author of *Orchos Tzaddikim* makes a brief statement which warrants an elaborate explanation. *"Envy stems from deficiency of soul."* This is equally true of desire. Let me use an example from medicine. The body requires certain essential nutrients. If any of these is missing, a "deficiency syndrome" results. If a person is lacking iron, this results in an "iron deficiency syndrome." Similarly, there are syndromes of "vitamin B deficiency" and "vitamin C deficiency," among others. Each deficiency syndrome has specific symptoms which alert the doctor to the condition, and laboratory tests can confirm the diagnosis.

Just as the body requires its essential nutrients, so does the *neshamah* (soul) require its essential nutrients. For Jews, these are the fulfillment of the 613 Scriptural mitzvos and their rabbinic derivatives, and refinement of *middos*. For non-Jews, it is the fulfillment of the Noahide mitzvos. Dereliction in providing the *neshamah* with its essential nutrients results in a " spiritual deficiency syndrome" which is every bit as real as the physical deficiency syndromes.

The principal symptom of the spiritual deficiency syndrome is *discontent*. This is not the same as "clinical depression," which is most often a biochemical disorder. Rather, there is a nondescript feeling of dissatisfaction which is nagging and persistent. Inasmuch as there is no laboratory test for this condition, and since discontent is a vague symptom, the correct diagnosis is most frequently overlooked.

The discontented individual understandably looks for relief from this most annoying feeling, and may reach out for anything that he thinks may provide relief. He may find temporary relief in alcohol or other mood-altering chemicals. If he finds that food soothes his discomfort, he may develop an eating disorder. He is vulnerable to any addictive condition. He may find that making money or the fulfillment of any physical craving gives him some relief. Inasmuch as none of these provide the missing essential nutrient, the relief is *ephemeral*, and the discontent soon recurs. He then repeats his relief-seeking behavior, which often results in habituation.

Some people may say, "I am strictly observant of all the mitzvos, so I cannot be spiritually deficient. Yet, I am constantly discontented."

I suspect that the failure of performance of mitzvos to relieve a spirituality deficiency syndrome is because these mitzvos are performed out of rote, with little investment of feeling. The Torah says, "You should love G-d with all your heart, with all your soul and with all your resources" (*Deuteronomy* 6:5). "To serve Him with all your heart and with all your soul" (ibid. 11:13). Let us be forthright. Our prayers are rarely with all our heart and all our soul. The prophet states, "They honor me with their mouths, but their hearts are distant from me" (*Isaiah* 29:13). Only a wholehearted devotion to mitzvos will relieve the discontent of spiritual deficiency. A profound study of the works of *mussar* and *chassidus*, and a sincere effort to perform mitzvos according to their full meanings, is necessary to overcome discontent.

It is easy for a person to blame the discontent on anything or anyone. Some people may think that they are displeased because of their job, their community or their spouse. In the hope of escaping the discontent, people have changed jobs, moved to another city, divorced, remarried or tried anything they thought might make them feel better. Alas! None of these maneuvers produces anything more than a very temporary respite.

It is tragic to see some people spend an entire lifetime in futile attempts to escape the misery of chronic discontent. The thought that they may be suffering from spiritual deficiency may not even occur to them.

We can understand why envy and desire can remove a person from the world. The envious person thinks that by gratifying his envy or desires he will be relieved of his discontent. However, it is like trying to fill a bottomless pit. A person may expend all his energy and make ruinous decisions in the wake of pursuing relief by these means.

The pursuit of acclaim is similarly futile. This drive is invariably due to feelings of low self-esteem. I addressed this problem at length in *Angels Don't Leave Footprints* and *Life's Too Short*. I described low self-esteem as being the product of *unwarranted* feelings of inadequacy, incompetence and worthlessness. These feelings may occur in people who are very gifted. A person with low self-esteem may seek recognition and acclaim in order to escape his discomfort. However, since these feelings have no basis in reality, the relief provided by acclaim is short-lived, and the pursuit is renewed. One man who had achieved many awards for community activities said, "I have an entire wall full of honorary plaques. They mean nothing to me."

A life rich in spirituality can provide healthy contentment and a feeling of worthiness. True, a person may and should feel that there is still much more he can do to advance himself spiritually, but this does not result in discontent. The Talmud says that "Envy of the wise increases one's wisdom" (*Bava Basra* 21a). Pursuit of wisdom and spirituality, too, may have no end point, but these pursuits do not ruin a person. To the contrary, they produce the nutrients which can provide lasting contentment.

Worry, Stress and Anxiety

I t is unimaginable that there was ever a time when people were free of worry, stress and anxiety. But although these are hardly new phenomena, they are undoubtedly more accentuated now.

We have noted that the goal of the *yetzer hara* is to render a person unable to fulfill his mission on earth. Although stress and worry occur normally, and even anxiety may have a constructive role, the *yetzer hara* exploits these for its purpose.

Stress serves a purpose. If one were not stressed to earn a living, one might just lie in bed all day. The natural state of all matter, including living things, is *inertia*. It is stress that makes one overcome inertia and do things. This is normal, healthy stress.

Unhealthy stress is when our energies are overtaxed. But even excessive demands on our energies would not be too harmful if they were not accompanied by internal stress, which is comprised of worry and anxiety.

Worry, too, can be healthy. If one is worried about how one will provide for his family, he will take the necessary steps to earn a living. If a student is worried about getting a good grade on his exam, he will be more diligent in his studies. Worry that can lead to constructive action is healthy.

Toxic worry is when there is nothing one can do about a situation, as for example, when a student has handed in his exam and worries that he may not get a good grade. Whereas worry before the exam may result in better preparation, worry after the exam is futile.

We often think, "What will happen if ... ?" If we can develop a contingency plan, then worrying about what might occur is constructive. If there is nothing one can do should a particular event happen, then worrying about it is worthless and toxic.

Examples of the two types of worry are legion. If one is concerned that one might get the flu, one gets immunized. That is constructive worry. If there is no vaccine available, worrying that one might get the flu cannot be of any help. To the contrary, worry that is futile may result in sleeplessness, poor appetite and lowering of the immune system and one's resistance. Such worrying may make one more vulnerable to the flu.

Much of the worry, stress and anxiety that has followed the terrorist attack on the World Trade Center was of the toxic variety. The government must take the necessary measures to prevent terrorist attacks, but there is little that an individual can do. Of course, one may avoid flying, entering tall buildings, driving through tunnels or over bridges or be near whatever one thinks may be a terrorist target. Most people, however, will not want to be so curtailed. If one continues to live normally, and is periodically reminded of the threat of terrorism by a "high alert" declaration, the worry of a terrorist attack lingers on. The *yetzer hara* can make use of this to throw a person into a state of constant tension if not despair.

In our discussion of anger we noted that the body prepares itself for a confrontation by undergoing a number of physiologic changes. These are referred to as constituting the "flight or fight" reaction. Among them are increased heart rate and respiration, a shift of the blood away from the digestive organs and body surface to the muscles, elevation of the blood sugar and some hormonal changes. These physiologic changes are advantageous in the event of a bodily attack, where "fighting or fleeing" are appropriate.

Many of these changes may occur with worry and tension , but there is nothing to fight and nowhere to flee. The body may remain as if in a constant state of preparedness for an attack, even if only subliminally. This may drain one's energies and impair concentration, which is precisely what the *yetzer hara* wishes to accomplish.

The Talmud says that the *yetzer hara* renews itself, grows in strength everyday and wishes to destroy a person (*Kiddushin* 30b, *Succah* 52a). This can be taken literally. By amplifying worry and tension, the *yetzer hara* can disable a person. We generally think of the *yetzer hara* only in terms of tempting a person to sin, which constitutes spiritual destruction. The *yetzer hara* may also destroy a person physically.

There are several things that can minimize tension. First of all, we should not overexpose ourselves unnecessarily to stress stimuli. On the days following the World Trade Center attack, many people watched the scene on television numerous times. For what purpose? This seems to be much like the tendency to touch a painful area, even though the touch may elicit pain.

We wish to be in touch with the latest happenings. Listening to or watching one morning and one evening newscast is enough. Nothing is gained by listening to newscasts multiple times a day. One should not listen to or watch newscasts during mealtime nor shortly before bedtime.

The Talmud states that the assault of the *yetzer hara* can be so severe that without the help of G-d one could not withstand it (ibid.). We must pray to G-d for His help.

Some may ask: Inasmuch as G-d allowed a disaster to

occur, why pray to Him for relief? I will repeat here what I have written elsewhere.

> *In a pediatrician's office, a mother sat with her year- old infant whom she had brought for his third immunization injection. The child was smiling and playing happily with toys, but when the white-clad doctor emerged, the child emitted a bloodcurdling shriek and clung to its mother for dear life. The child remembered previous episodes only too well. He saw this white-clad person as a fiend who hurts him, stabbing him with a sharp weapon and causing him to be sick for two days.*

> *When the mother took the child into the treatment room for the shot and restrained him, the child cried, kicked and clawed his mother. Certainly, the child could not understand why his mother, who always cared for him and loved him, had now turned traitor and collaborated with this evil monster to hurt him.*

> *After the doctor administered the injection and left the room, the child threw his arms around the mother and held her tightly. But why was he turning to her for security? Wasn't she the one who had participated in the attack and collaborated with the enemy?*

> *Although the child was unable to understand his mother's behavior, he nevertheless knew that she loved him and would care for him. She would look after him and comfort him during the two-day reaction that often follows immunization.*

The gap between our mortal minds and the infinite wisdom of G-d is greater than that between the infant's mind and his mother's wisdom. Although we have no inkling of why G-d allows bad things to happen, we know that He loves us and cares for us. Like the infant, we turn to Him for security. This is why we should pray to G-d for help in stressful times.

It is also important to increase friendship ties and stay close with family and friends. The popular aphorism, "Troubles shared with others is halved," can be found in the *Sefer HaChinuch*, 331.

The more we refine our *middos* and observe mitzvos, the closer we will feel to G-d, and the better we will be able to tolerate stress.

I said that even anxiety can be healthy. An example of this is the anxiety that precedes a wedding, where the parents maybe anxious that the invitations might not be ready on time, and that something might be overlooked in the wedding preparations. This anxiety causes them to prod the printer and check with the caterer. As with worry, anxiety that results in accomplishing something is not harmful.

Traumatic events are not the only causes of tension. As our technology has resulted in unprecedented high-speed communication, our level of patience and tolerance has dropped precipitously. People expect things to happen instantaneously, and there may be greater pressure to deliver services and goods immediately.

While we should do our best to accommodate and avoid procrastinating, we should avoid becoming victims of pressure. If we say, in a calm tone, "Yes, I know you want it delivered immediately. I assure you I will do my best to do so," we will actually help others become more patient. By the same token, when we are on the receiving end, we should exercise patience. It is especially important not to allow things to go unattended until the last moment, and then rush to meet a deadline. Judicious planning can help avoid much tension.

It is especially important to maintain a calm attitude within the home. The Talmud says that on Friday afternoon, one should check with family members whether all the necessary preparations for Shabbos have been made. However, the Talmud cautions, one should say this in a calm, non-threatening tone, so that everyone will comply (*Shabbos* 34a). In general, the Talmud exhorts one never to instill fear in the home by making dictatorial demands (*Gittin* 6b).

In the workplace, we may be pressured to get things done quickly, and we may pass this pressure on to others. Occasionally, it may be unavoidable to issue sharp orders to others at work; however, we must be most cautious not to bring such attitudes home. A peaceful home environment is one of the most effective antidotes to toxic stress. Maintaining an attitude of patience, tolerance and calm within the home can make life more pleasant for everyone.

Many people take for granted that they know how to relax, but this may not be true. Do a simple experiment. Lean back on in a comfortable recliner in a dimly lit room, with neither the radio, television, or stereo operating. Close your eyes and breathe regularly. Many people find that they get restless after just two minutes of such "relaxation." They feel they need to read, listen to something, or do something in order to relax. What they are actually doing then is "diverting" themselves, but not really relaxing.

We should learn to relax. There are instructive books on relaxation techniques. An excellent text is *The Relaxation Response* by Dr. Herbert Benson. Proper and judicious relaxation may relieve many of the symptoms resulting from anxiety and excessive stress.

11
The Cult of Productivity

The driving force in Western civilization is *productivity*. The economy is based on productivity, and unfortunately, values are often assigned to people based on their productivity. We are creatures of habit and are profoundly influenced by our environment. Inasmuch as we spend so much of the day at work, we may take on the prevailing doctrine of the workplace and allow it to affect our personal lives.

Value in commerce is determined by the "bottom line." Profit is good, loss is bad. A person who goes into a business venture with reckless abandon, ignoring every bit of good judgment and doing things which portend doom, yet ends up with a windfall profit is considered a hero in the business world. He is a "good" businessman. On the other hand, someone who begins a venture based on sound business principles and with the finest intentions but rapidly goes into bankruptcy is considered a schlemiel. He is a "bad" businessman. People will invest their money with business people who can turn a profit, not with those who go bankrupt. Good and bad are determined by outcome.

While this attitude may be appropriate in commerce, it has no place in our personal lives. There are many factors that determine how a child will develop, and many of these are beyond parental control. Parents should do the best they can, seeking guidance and striving to raise their children to be honest and productive. How the children will turn out is beyond their control.

We pray to the G-d of Abraham, Isaac and Jacob. G-d says of Abraham, "For I have loved him, because he instructs his children and his household after him that they keep the way of G-d" (*Genesis* 18:19). Yet of Abraham's eight sons (v. *Genesis* 25:2), only Isaac continued Abraham's legacy. But G-d loved Abraham, because he did the best he could. No parent, even the Patriarch Abraham, can control results. Isaac and Rebecca certainly tried their best to raise both their children properly, yet only Jacob was righteous. King Hezekiah was a *tzaddik*, although there is no question that his father, Ahaz, who was a sinner, did not instruct his son in the way of Torah.

The ethical correctness of any act is determined by the intent and purpose for which it was done. If an avaricious surgeon would perform an unnecessary operation and happen to find an unsuspected cancer which he removed, he may have indeed saved the patient's life, but he is an unethical surgeon. If a surgeon agonized whether to perform an operation, consulted other specialists and discussed the risks with the patient and family, and then decided that the patient's best chance for survival was with surgery, he is an ethical doctor even if the surgery was unsuccessful and the patient died. We have no control over outcome. We can control only our actions. The principles determining right and wrong in personal life are radically different than those of commerce.

But the *yetzer hara* exploits the prevailing commercial principles in which we are immersed most of our waking hours, and uses them to crush us. When things do not turn out the way we had planned, it makes us consider ourselves as failures, incompetent and inadequate. It throws us into a state of dejection, and achieves its goal in disabling us.

We are so influenced by the prevailing principles that we may allow them to affect our study of Torah. It is not uncommon that a student of Torah may fail to understand something he is studying. The *yetzer hara* seizes the opportunity to say, "Your study of Torah is of little use. You can't understand it anyway. You might as well close the books and do something more productive." The response to the *yetzer hara* should be, "The mitzvah is not necessarily that one must *understand* Torah. The mitzvah is to *study* Torah, and that is what I will continue to do."

Because of the current cultural obsession with productivity and results, it is more than ever necessary to remember the Talmudic statements: "It is not incumbent upon you to complete the task, but neither are you free to refrain from doing it" (*Ethics of the Fathers* 2:21) and "If a person attempted to do a mitzvah but was unable to do so because of circumstances beyond his control, G-d considers it as if he had in fact done it" (*Berachos* 6a).

This attack by the *yetzer hara* is a new phenomenon. People in the *shtetl* worked for a living, but they were not saturated with commercialism. A person today may be meticulously observant of all the mitzvos, yet may be unaware that the *yetzer hara* has trapped him into applying his workday standards to the nonbusiness aspects of his life. The cult of productivity and its profound influence on us points out why regular study of *mussar* is so crucial.

Communication and Information

Historians and archeologists speak of "the stone age," the "iron age" or the "bronze age." How will future historians refer to our era? I believe they will call it "the information age" or "the communication age." Technology has advanced communication to undreamed-of heights. What was once the miraculous rapid transmission of the telegraph is now a historic relic. Fax machines deliver documents instantaneously, and e-mail can transmit volumes with the speed of light. Telephones with a variety of modalities allow committees as well as individuals to converse. It is common to see people walking on the street or driving a car while communicating with someone by cellular telephone. Via virtual television, I have lectured to and interacted with audiences across the Atlantic and Pacific Oceans.

Much the same is true of information. A few CD-ROM discs can place a whole library of information at one's fingertips. The abundance of data that is readily available to everyone has resulted in information overload for people who do not pick and choose. Communication and information advances within the past few decades have revolutionized the world.

These marvelous advances have not failed to leave their mark. Just as subliminal advertising can impact upon one's mind without one being aware of it, so can changes in life styles influence us without our even being aware of it.

Increased "knowing and sharing" are the side effects of communication and information. But "knowing and sharing" are also the two components of the most grievous of all sins, *lashon hara*. We now have access to much more information about people, and we can easily transmit it instantaneously across the globe via telephone and e-mail. A negative comment about a person can be typed out, and with the touch of a finger transmitted electronically to numerous people in one's e-mail address book.

Years ago it would have taken much time and effort to convey a juicy piece of gossip from the United States to Israel. Whatever the "kick" one might have gotten from sharing gossip was just not worth the time and effort it took. This is no longer true.

The Talmud says of *lashon hara* that it can kill the object of the gossip, and that whereas an arrow can kill only someone in the proximity, *lashon hara* can kill over a long distance. How prophetic their words were!

The gravity of *lashon hara* is spelled out clearly in halachah, yet none of our great Torah scholars throughout the generations found it necessary to devote volumes to this subject. The fact that just in the past generation the Chafetz Chaim did devote entire volumes to the elucidation and gravity of *lashon hara* was because he realized that it had become much more prevalent. Our generation is even more susceptible to this sin.

The Chafetz Chaim worked tirelessly to impress people that words and even gestures can be lethal weapons, because many people may give little substance to words. However small the understanding of this concept was in his time, it has shrunk to microscopic size now. The Talmud says that when a forbidden act is committed several times, it loses its opprobrium and is considered permissible (*Yoma* 86b). By exploiting the fallout from the advances of "the communication and information age," that facilitate *lashon hara,* the *yetzer hara* has been victorious in causing more people to commit this grievous sin.

Simple solutions are not enough. Stickers affixed to telephones that read "Don't speak *lashon hara*" are not very effective. I saw someone pick up a receiver with such a sticker and proceed to spew *lashon hara.* The problem is that people may not realize that what they are saying is *lashon hara.* It is amazing how people can justify spreading gossip.

Because of the prevalence of *lashon hara* there is no option other than to continue the work of the Chafetz Chaim. Rabbis should give frequent instructions on what constitutes *lashon hara* and should dispel the erroneous notions wherewith people justify speaking *lashon hara.* Teachers in yeshivos and seminaries should reinforce their teaching about *lashon hara.* Rabbis should point out in their sermons that children are being taught about the gravity of *lashon hara*, and that if parents speak *lashon hara* they may lose the respect of their children.

Whereas we do not know what are the specific consequences of any sin, there is one exception: *lashon hara.* The Midrash makes a startling statement. The generation of King Ahab was ridden with the grievous sin of idolatry. Yet, they were triumphant in battle *because they did not speak lashon hara.* On the other hand, the generation of King David were *tzaddikim,* yet their soldiers fell in battle *because there was lashon hara among them* (*Vayikra Rabbah* 26:2). No doubt the generation of David merited *Gan Eden* and the generation of Ahab descended to *Gehinnom.* It is not for us to understand why, but the above Midrash tells us that the safety of the soldiers who defend Israel is contingent on our avoidance of *lashon hara.* If people were made aware of this, the thought that their careless talk may jeopardize the safety of a Jewish soldier would heighten their alertness and discourage *lashon hara.*

The telephone showed us how far words can travel. The computers that can write out the spoken word show us that words are more than just sound waves received by the ear. Words are actually concrete substances that can have a permanent existence. We can use this lesson of technology to turn the table of the *yetzer hara's* exploitation of technology for its nefarious purpose, become more aware and sensitive, and strengthen our avoidance of *lashon hara.*

13

Finding Joy in Life

From earlier writings, it is evident that there was always a problem in achieving *simchah* (joy). But the dire warnings (*Deuteronomy* 28:47) of what would befall us if we did not serve G-d in times of *simchah* did not have to be of such great concern then. Why? Because Moses' rebuke was if one did not serve G-d "with gladness and goodness of heart, *when everything was abundant.*" The lack of *simchah* throughout much of our history did not have to be attributed to the machinations of the *yetzer hara*. There were not too many periods in Jewish history "when everything was abundant" and when circumstances were very conducive for *simchah.*

The writings of the Baal Shem Tov and his followers stress the importance of developing *simchah*. This was not necessarily because there was a struggle with the *yetzer hara*. Rather, the conditions of life in the 17th century for most of the Jews in eastern Europe were deplorable. They were deprived of civil rights, were not permitted to live in the cities, and in the villages they were under the despotic rule of anti-Semitic *poritzim* (feudal lords) who often incited pogroms. Many lived in poverty, and many did not have access to education. Infant mortality, childhood diseases and tuberculosis ravaged the population.

In the centuries prior to that, the Crusades and the Inquisition resulted in massacres. Little wonder that it required great effort to generate *simchah*. The *yetzer hara* did not have to do anything to bring about an attitude of dejection. It was spontaneous. The reprimand of Moses could hardly apply to these people.

But the absence of *simchah* today cannot be attributed to these factors. Jews in the United States enjoy equal rights, and are well represented in the professions. While there certainly are Jews who live in poverty, most can enjoy at least a reasonable standard of life. Infant mortality is rare, and immunization has eliminated most childhood diseases. Tuberculosis is no longer a killer of young people, and the average life span is 80 years.

In my childhood, it was difficult for observant Jews to find jobs that did not require working on Shabbos. Today, *shomer Shabbos* jobs and businesses are common. Kosher products are easily available, as are fast foods and a variety of ethnic cuisine. With so much of the discomfort removed, the absence of *simchah* today generally cannot be attributed to unfavorable circumstances, and can only be the work of the *yetzer hara*, and this is why we must find ways of combating it.

Why is the *yetzer hara* so interested in preventing one from feeling *simchah*? Because *simchah* is the attitude most conducive for sincere service of G-d. As was noted earlier, the goal of the *yetzer hara* is to disable a person, and depressing a person's spirits can achieve this. It is now, more than ever before, that we must apply the teachings in the Torah literature on how to thwart the *yetzer hara's* efforts to prevent us from having *simchah*.

What is the key to *simchah*? It is not, as many people think, amassing great fortunes or enjoying luxurious comforts. These are fleeting pleasures. King Solomon has pointed out how empty these really are. "All that is under the sun is worthless" (*Ecclesiastes* 1:14), which our sages have interpreted to mean that only that which is *above* the sun, i.e., celestial and spiritual, is of true value.

I must repeat here what I have written elsewhere, a story my father often told.

> In the days of feudalism, a cruel poritz (feudal lord) sentenced one of his vassals to twenty-five years of hard labor. The man's hands were shackled to the handle of a giant wheel attached to the wall, and all day he had to turn this massive wheel. He would try to imagine what it was that he was accomplishing. Perhaps he was grinding grain into flour, or perhaps he was bringing up water from a deep well to irrigate the fields.
>
> After the twenty-five years finally came to an end and the shackles were removed, the man promptly ran to the other side of the wall. He emitted a painful cry and fell dead. The wheel was not attached to anything! For twenty-five years he had suffered backbreaking pain, all for nothing! Neither man nor beast had benefited from his gruesome labor.

My father repeatedly pointed out that the most depressing feeling a person can suffer is *futility*. We can withstand much distress if only we know that it serves a purpose.

Enjoying delicacies or pastimes may indeed be pleasant, but we cannot believe that these achieve an ultimate purpose. Even if we delude ourselves consciously, our subconscious is not deceived. We have a gnawing feeling that our lives may be futile. True, we may seek to escape this tormenting feeling by engaging in some ephemeral pleasure, but the depressing feeling that our lives may be futile persists.

True meaning in life can be only in that which is "above the sun," spiritual and celestial. This is why our Torah writings speak of *simchah shel mitzvah*, the joy of fulfilling the Divine commandments. As was pointed out earlier, these are the nutrients of the *neshamah*, and these alone can provide enduring happiness.

It is unfortunate that we so often fail to derive *simchah* from the performance of mitzvos. Yes, we do them, and we may even do them in the most meticulous way. But how often do our faces glow with happiness after we have given *tzedakah*, listened to the shofar, put on *tefillin*, or said the blessing after meals?

One Passover morning I was on my way to shul. In front of me was a young man who was walking his dog and whistling merrily. At one point, he snapped his fingers and turned around in a little dance. He was clearly in a happy mood.

I thought, *What is wrong with me that I am not jumping for joy? Last night I had the good fortune to perform so many mitzvos! I davened in the evening, recited kiddush, read the Haggadah to fulfill the commandment of recalling our libera-tion from the enslavement in Egypt and the many wonders of the Exodus, ate the matzah and the maror (bitter herbs), and conducted the entire Seder, so many ways in which I fulfilled G-d's wishes, yet this has not caused me to feel so elated that I should be dancing in joy, unable to contain my emotion. This young man in front of me is happy, probably because at the moment he does not have a care in the world. But I have so much more to be ecstatically happy about, yet I feel nothing!* Something was wrong.

I suspect that I am not alone in this. I do not see many people being euphoric because of doing mitzvos. But if we would only give proper thought to the words of the *berachos* we recite before doing mitzvos, we might well feel elated. "G-d has made us holy with His mitzvos." Each mitzvah is a step closer to a relationship with the *Melech Ha'Olom,* Sovereign of the Universe.

If a person was given a ticket to attend the inauguration of the President of the United States, one would feel privileged. The closer one's seat is to the ceremonial podium, the more one would feel honored, and undoubtedly very happy. That is why we should feel happy and privileged in coming closer to G-d by doing His mitzvos.

It is the nature of all living things to grow. Our physical growth is completed by the end of our second decade, but our spiritual growth should continue indefinitely. If we frustrate our growth, we are spiritually stunted. Maharal states that the name for man, Adam, is derived from the word *adamah* (earth). The earth has the potential to make things grow, and this potential is integral to man. Failure to grow is, therefore, a denial of the very essence of man (*Tiferes Yisrael* 3).

Rabbi Samson Raphael Hirsch points out that the Hebrew word *same'ach* (= happy), is closely related to the word *tzome'ach* (= growing). This is because human happiness is contingent on spiritual growth. If we fail to feel the joy of mitzvos, it is because we are unaware that mitzvos make us grow.

It is related that shortly before his death, the Gaon of Vilna wept. He said that he was sad to leave a world where for just a few pennies one can perform the mitzvah of *tzitzis,* which can assure one of greeting the Divine Presence. Indeed, he would have a lofty place in Gan Eden (Paradise), but there is no further growth in Gan Eden.

The Maggid of Mezeritch said that one of the things we should learn from an infant is that it is virtually always happy. The happiness of an infant may well be because it is rapidly growing. Each day brings new understanding, new words and new abilities. The infant is constantly looking to discover new things in its surroundings.

As we noted, the most profound depression results from not having any real achievement. Growing spiritually by performing mitzvos is true achievement, and this should give us boundless joy. Maharal states that just as sorrow is the result of loss, *simchah* is the result of completion. When we strive to achieve our completion, we experience *simchah* (*Derech Chaim* 6:2).

The *simchah* that should emanate from performance of mitzvos is predicated on the conviction that G-d created man for purpose and gave us the Torah and mitzvos whereby we can fulfill that purpose. The quality of *simchah* one derives from performance of mitzvos corresponds to the degree of one's *emunah*, belief in the basic premise of Judaism. If we do not experience *simchah* in performance of mitzvos, we must strive to improve the quality of our *emunah*. This, of course, is one of the major battles with the *yetzer hara,* which uses every possible stratagem to subvert our *emunah.*

Another key to *simchah* is to be content with what one has, as the Talmud says, "Who is wealthy? One who is happy with his lot" (*Ethics of the Fathers* 4:1). We have noted that dissatisfaction with one's lot and pursuit of wealth is frustrating because there is no end point with which one will be contented.

We may not be able to achieve the level of spirituality of R' Zusia of Anipole, who was always happy in spite of his abject poverty. When asked how he could recite in good faith the *berachah* thanking G-d for "providing me with all my needs" when he was in fact lacking so much, R' Zusia said, "G-d knows my needs better than I do. He knows that one of my needs is poverty, so He has given me what I need." But if we cannot aspire to the extraordinary spiritual height of being happy when one is destitute, we should nevertheless be content with what we have, rather than constantly aspire for more and more.

One of the sharpest reprimands I have ever received came from a patient who had been sober for several months.

> I had just acquired a new automobile, "loaded" with state-of-the-art extras. I was very frustrated to find that the "cruise control" was not accurate. Taking the car to the mechanic to have it adjusted would be time consuming.
>
> That day the newly recovering patient told me how happy she was that she was able to find a minimum wage job which would enable her to get a better apartment. "I might also save enough money to repair my car."
>
> "What's wrong with your car?" I asked.
>
> "It does not have a reverse gear," she said.
>
> "How can you drive without a reverse gear?" I asked.
>
> "You have to be more careful, especially when parking, to know how you're going to get out. But I have to remember that there are people who don't have any car at all," she said.
>
> I had properly been put in my place. Because the cruise control was not precise I was dissatisfied with a new automobile that had everything, while this woman considered herself to be fortunate even though her car could not go in reverse.

Discontent is often the result of feeling that one has been deprived of one's due. If we can feel that G-d has given us what we need and we do not feel deprived, we can be content and happy. This is evident from David's statement: "A song of thanksgiving: Call out to G-d, everyone on earth. Serve G-d with gladness, come before Him with joyous song ... We are His people and the sheep of His pasture. Enter His gates with thanksgiving" (*Psalm* 100). Gratitude and joy are coupled.

Gratitude requires an awareness that one is indebted to another for a favor one received. People who are fiercely self-sufficient and cannot accept anything from anyone cannot be grateful. Our awareness that we are dependent on G-d enables us to be thankful, and the knowledge that "We are His people and the sheep of His pasture," and that G-d cares for us like a shepherd cares for his flock, enables us to be content with what He has given us. With discontent eliminated, we can feel joy.

The importance of gratitude is stressed by R' Meir Rubman, who cites the verse "There arose a new king in Egypt who did not know Joseph" (*Exodus* 1:8), and the opinion in the Talmud that this was not actually a new king, but the old king who denied knowledge of Joseph (*Sotah* 11a).

Rabbi Rubman points out that Pharaoh had been enormously indebted to Joseph, who not only saved the country from a catastrophic famine, but also brought unprecedented wealth into the royal treasury. His response to Joseph's interpretation to his dream was, "Since G-d has informed you of all this, there can be no one so discerning and wise as you" (*Genesis* 41:39). Yet, when Moses appealed to him in the name of G-d to allow the Israelites to leave for three days to worship him in the desert, Pharaoh said, "Who is G-d that I should heed to His voice? I do not know G-d, nor will I send out the Israelites" (*Exodus* 5:2). Rabbi Rubman says that *ingratitude toward another person leads to denial of G-d.* Conversely, one of the fundamentals that brings one to an acknowledgment of G-d is to acknowledge one's gratitude to other people (*Lekach Tov Exodus* p.5).

While saying "thank you" should not be an ordeal, it is interesting to note that even small children are reluctant to say these two words. Mother may tell the child, "Say 'thank you' to the nice man for the candy,' and as often as not, the child may turn away with a grunt. Even a child may feel that to feel and acknowledge gratitude may cause him to feel beholden. No one, not even a small child, likes to feel beholden to others.

The resistance to acknowledging gratitude is discussed in the Talmud, which states that Moses reprimanded the Israelites for being ingrates. When they heard the voice of G-d at Sinai, they said that it was too awesome for them to hear, and they asked Moses to convey G-d's words to them. G-d approved of this and said, "Who would give that they should always have this reverence for Me ... ?" (*Deuteronomy* 5:25-26). Moses said to them, "You should have responded to G-d, '*You* should give us this feeling of reverence so that we should always be in awe of You.' You are ingrates for not having asked G-d for this."

In what way did this make them ingrates? Tosafos explains that they did not want to ask this of G-d *because they did not want to feel beholden to Him* (*Avodah Zarah* 7a). The psychology of reluctance to feel and express gratitude is contained in two lines of Tosafos!

This helps us understand a rather puzzling Talmudic statement. The Talmud says that the reason the Second Temple was destroyed, even though the Jews were observant of Torah study, *avodah* (Divine service) and *gemilas chasadim* (acts of kindness), is because there was *sinas chinam* (unwarranted dislike). The obvious question is: If they were so observant of *gemilas chasadim* and did acts of kindness for others, where could there have been dislike? The answer is that those who were the *recipients* of acts of kindness were guilty of unwarranted dislike, because in their reluctance to feel obligated and beholden to their benefactors, not only did they fail to express gratitude, but they also developed *resentments* toward those who had been kind to them. This was the *sinas chinam*.

As pointed out by Moses, we cannot enjoy G-d's bounty if we are unable to appreciate it and be thankful to Him.

In summary, *simchah* is primarily an issue of *emunah*. The stronger our trust in G-d and our conviction that He will provide us with what we really need, the more likely we will be content with what we have, and our *simchah* will not be compromised by discontent. The greater our realization that observing mitzvos will elevate us spiritually and bring us closer to the fulfillment of the purpose of our existence, the greater our *simchah* can be.

One may ask: If all our joy is to be derived from spiritual advancement, what is the role of enjoyment from earthly pleasures? Rabbeinu Yonah says that judicious partaking of worldly pleasures allows a person to exercise and fulfill one's spiritual potential (*Vehayisa Ach Same'ach* Jerusalem, 1989, p. 16). We may better understand this with a parable of the Baal Shem Tov.

> The Baal Shem Tov was asked whether the physical pleasures of Shabbos are not inconsistent with its spiritual character.
>
> "Not all," the Baal Shem Tov said, and he related the following parable.
>
> A prince was exiled from the palace to a distant land for having committed an offense. After a number of years, he received notification that he was pardoned and could return to the palace. He was so overjoyed that he wished to celebrate his good fortune by song and dance. However, onlookers who did not know of his circumstances might think him deranged if he sang and danced. He, therefore, went to an inn where villagers gathered, and treated them to a sumptuous meal with abundant drink. When they became a bit inebriated, the villagers arose to sing and dance, and this gave the prince the opportunity to sing and dance with them without appearing conspicuous.
>
> "So it is with the celebration of Shabbos," the Baal Shem Tov said. "The soul wishes to rejoice in the spirituality of Shabbos, but the body cannot participate in spiritual delight. We, therefore, give the body delicacies which it can enjoy. A person can, therefore,

be happy on Shabbos. He gives the body something to enjoy so that it does not stand in the way of the soul's celebrating spiritual delights."

While the parable is appropriate, we should realize that if the prince would allow himself to be carried away with the revelry of the villagers, his good intentions would soon come to naught as he would descend to their level. Similarly, although Rabbeinu Yonah says that *judicious* worldly pleasures have a place, we must beware that these do not lead to indulgence.

Spiritual growth is not spontaneous. The Midrash states that over each blade of grass there stands an angel that commands it to grow. Why is this necessary? The seed has all the requisite nutrients for growth in the earth. Will growth not take place spontaneously? The message of the Midrash is that the natural state of all matter is *inertia.* Any change, including growth, must overcome the resistance of inertia even if all the circumstances conducive to growth are present.

צומח, t*zome'ach,* and שמח, *same'ach.* True joy can come only from spiritual growth. To merit true joy, we must be willing to invest effort.

If we consider all these factors, we should indeed feel joy. Anytime we find ourselves feeling despondent in absence of actual losses, we should know that this is nothing but the *yetzer hara* at work to prevent us from feeling joy in life and render us dysfunctional in fulfilling the Divine will, the ultimate goal in life. We should reject such feelings of sadness just as we reject the *yetzer hara* when it urges us to commit any flagrant Torah violation.

The Sandwich Generation

Having identified the *yetzer hara* as a mortal foe, it is only logical that it will seek to attack where it can do the greatest damage. One such area is the respect of parents. The Talmud says that when children respect their parents, G-d says, "I consider it as though I were dwelling among them and they were respecting Me" (*Kiddushin* 30). Disrespect of parents is tantamount to disrespect of G-d.

Inasmuch as we are concerned with the *yetzer hara's* operation in modern times, why is there any need to address this issue? Parent-child relationships have been in existence since time immemorial.

Conditions today are radically different than just several decades ago. Medical science is constantly advancing the average life span. In the first half of the past century the average life span was 40. Now it is 80 and rising. Many more people have elderly parents. Yet, medical progress in curing the wear-and-tear diseases of later life has not kept pace with the increase in longevity. People are indeed living longer, but are still prone to arthritis, stroke, impairment of vision and hearing, and perhaps the most dreaded of all diseases of the elderly, Alzheimer's disease.

The losses of memory and orientation in Alzheimer's disease are particularly devastating, often necessitating round-the-clock observation. This problem is much more formidable today than it was in the *shtetl*. A number of years ago I came upon a scene in one of the quieter neighborhoods in Jerusalem. An elderly woman had wandered away from her home and could not find her way back. One of the neighbors saw her and took her back home. This was possible in a neighborhood where everyone was familiar with everyone else and knew where they lived. This could not happen in a modern urban area, especially where there is danger of the elderly person wandering into busy traffic.

Depending on a variety of circumstances, including finances, living conditions for the elderly may vary. Some may be fortunate in being totally independent, others may require some help in the home, others may require assisted living facilities, and yet others may require a total care facility. In some situations the only practical option is for the parents to live with their children. This is especially true if one parent has died, where the other, even if physically capable of caring for himself or herself, is unable to tolerate the loneliness.

Younger people in their 40's whose children are adolescents and require parental attention may now also have to care for an elderly parent or parents who are living with them. The needs of the elderly parents may be much different than those of the children. The youngsters may wish to play their music at decibels which are annoying to the grandparents. They may dress in ways which the parents tolerate but the grandparents do not, and they rebuke them for it. Other conflicts may occur between the needs of the grandparents and those of the children. The parents, who feel an obligation toward both, are caught in the middle.

This has given rise to the parents being referred to as "the sandwich generation."

The situation becomes even more thorny when both parents must work to support the family. The time these parents have for their children is limited, and giving attention to the elderly parents detracts from the time they can devote to the children. Indeed, the pressure and demands from both ends of the spectrum may make the analogy to a vise more appropriate than to a sandwich.

The psychology section of the bookstore has a number of books dealing with the problem of "elder abuse." Such titles did not exist just several decades ago.

The strong tradition of parental respect in Judaism may cause people to think that abuse of the elderly cannot possibly occur in the Jewish community. That is just what was felt about alcoholism, drug addiction and domestic violence. It is time that we shed these delusions of immunity and recognize that we are vulnerable to all social diseases. The *yetzer hara* knows its business only too well. Given the overwhelming importance Torah ascribes to the mitzvah of respecting one's parents, it is understandable that the *yetzer hara* will choose this mitzvah as a target.

The *yetzer hara* is cunning, and can exploit the current attitude toward the elderly to affect children's feelings. What I am about to say may not be pleasant to hear, but there is no point in living in a make-believe world. We must know the facts if we are to make proper adjustments.

Earlier we noted that our society places great value on productivity. Like it or not, the fact that the elderly are no longer productive diminishes their value in modern society. If you pay close attention to the media, not a single day goes by without there being some mention of the economic burden resulting from the increasing number of people surviving to an old age, along with dire predictions (however concealed) that the number of elderly will progressively increase.

There is serious concern that the social security system will eventually not be solvent, and the concern is openly expressed by the younger, working population who are paying huge amounts into the system that by the time they are eligible, the cupboard will be bare. We are told that a major part of Medicare costs occur in the last six months of life. Some states have declined payment for certain medical procedures for people over 80. Not too long ago, euthanasia was widely regarded as murder. Today, several legislatures have legalized physician-assisted suicide.

I recall that when Medicare was in the planning phase during President Johnson's administration, there was a White House conference at which organized medicine voiced its opposition to the program. A government spokesperson said, "You doctors have no right to object to the program. You are the ones at fault for prolonging the lives of the elderly."

No one will be as brazen to openly voice such sentiments, but it is inescapable that the underlying attitude toward the elderly is not completely benign. In Oriental countries, the elderly are revered and held sacred. This is not so in Western civilization.

Although Jews, as are the Orientals, were traditionally guided by the Torah principle, "In the presence of an old person shall you rise and you shall honor the presence of the elderly" (*Leviticus* 19:32), we have not been impervious to the prevailing attitude. The *yetzer hara* exploits this attitude to affect the relationship to the elderly.

When one is in a "sandwich situation," with obligations both as a parent to one's children and a child to one's parents, one may feel being in the midst of a tug-of-war. Inasmuch as one does not have unlimited time, energy and resources, one may feel guilty regardless of what one does. One feels relatively neglectful of either one's parents, one's children, or both. It may be or seem like a "no-win" situation.

When a person has tried to do what is right to the best of one's ability, there is no reason to feel guilty. If one has in fact done something wrong, guilt is a healthy feeling that leads to the rectification of the wrong deed and the avoidance of its repetition. Unwarranted feelings of guilt are the work of the *yetzer hara*. The conflicting roles of caring for one's children and for one's parents can be a drain on one's energy. Add to this the issues of conscience, and the situation is ripe for agony.

The obvious questions are: "What is right and what is wrong? Who is the authority to render such a decision?"

The issues that arise in regard to parent care, whether they relate to the role of being both a parent or a child, or to being a caregiver while holding a job, are extremely complex. There are far too many variables to allow for any general guidelines. This book is not intended as a guide on relationships or for child-parent problems. Its purpose is to call attention to ethical problems that are relatively new, and for which we must seek clarification and develop appropriate coping techniques.

There are two sources of direction that a person has: the *yetzer tov* and the *yetzer hara*. The advice of the *yetzer tov* emanates from the principles of *tzedek* (righteousness). The advice of the *yetzer hara* emanates from the physical drives for pleasure and comfort. We are invariably biased by our emotions, which can distort our judgments.

The principles of *tzedek* are based on the Torah. The authority to render a decision on what one should do in the complex cases of parent care should be made by a *posek*, an acknowledged Torah scholar qualified to make halachic decisions. The *posek* must be given all the pertinent information, including not only the medical and social factors, but the family constellation as well. When one does what is halachically correct, one may experience various feelings, but none of these should be guilt.

The only way to thwart the interference of the yetzer hara in parent-care problems is to seek a halachic decision and to abide by it.

I came face-to-face with the complexity of parent-care problems on my first day in my psychiatric training. My first patient was a 58-year-old woman who was depressed. Here is her story.

Esther was the youngest of four, with three older brothers. When she was 28 and engaged to be married, her father suffered a stroke. Esther felt that her mother needed her help in caring for the invalid. She told her fiance that they could occupy the apartment above that of her parents, which would enable her to help her mother. Her fiance disapproved of this, feeling that it would detract from her relationship to him. He had no problem in providing money to secure necessary help, but did not wish to live in such close proximity. Esther broke the engagement.

Esther lived with her parents and continued to hold a job. When she was 40, her father died. Esther felt that her mother needed her companionship, and she remained with her mother. When Esther was 56, her mother died.

Many years earlier, Esther had been confronted with a difficult problem. What was the right thing to do? To marry and have a family would mean that her mother would have to carry the total burden of caring for her father, albeit hired help would be available. Should she marry and leave the home, or should she remain at home and forgo marriage? Esther opted for the latter, *but made the decision on her own.*

In the hospital, Esther said, "Look at me now. I always wanted children but have none. Who needs me? My brothers have gone their own way. What should I do now? I have no purpose for which to live."

I am not a *posek*, and had Esther consulted me when she was 28 I would not have been competent to make a halachic decision. There certainly may have been other factors in

Esther's depression, but there was no question that she was now in torment for having sacrificed her future and life to assist her mother in caring for her father.

We often make sacrifices in life, and sometimes very major sacrifices. The Patriarch Abraham had help in making the supreme sacrifice because he knew that obeying the will of G-d was right.

Esther agonized because she could not feel that she had done the right thing. Perhaps she should have married her betrothed and accepted his offer to secure help for her mother. She felt she missed out on what was so important to her — having and raising children — because she had made a wrong decision.

I cannot say what the right decision was. But if Esther would have had the comfort of knowing that she had done right in sacrificing her future to help her parents, she would not have been in such deep remorse. If an authoritative halachic decision would have been for her to marry, she could have done so without feeling guilty that she was abandoning her parents.

The problems that can arise for "the sandwich generation" are legion. In addition to the conflict between providing for the care of parents vs. children, there are numerous others. For example, should one quit work in order to look after a parent? Is it appropriate to go on vacation if this means turning over care of a parent to others? Is it legitimate for siblings to place the responsibility of care for a parent on one of the children? A parent is in a nursing home, and the son has an excellent job opportunity which will enable him to provide much better for his family. The job is in a distant city, and he will not be able to make weekly visits to the parent. Should he forgo the job opportunity? When grandparents make unreasonable demands of the grandchildren, should the latter be forced to comply, or should they be allowed to do things that aggrevate the grandparents?

Decisions in these kinds of problems may be influenced by factors other than doing what is ethically right. Competent and authoritative guidance is necessary.

Just as there are physicians who are general practitioners and others who are specialists, this is also true of halachic authorities. Although I am a physician and a board-certified psychiatrist, I cannot provide consultation or treatment for children or adolescents because I have not had the requisite training and experience for this age group. I must refer people to therapists with this expertise.

This is equally true for halachic authorities, who should render decisions only in their area of expertise. If the rabbi one consults has not had training in a particular area, he should refer to someone with the requisite expertise.

The Talmud quotes G-d as saying, "I created the *yetzer hara*, and I created the Torah as an antidote" (*Kiddushin* 30b). When we abide by authoritative halachic decisions, we can be free of the *yetzer hara's* disabling tactics.

I must share with you an anecdote which I believe has an important message, but first a word of explanation.

The ethicist, R' Shlomo Wolbe, says that the greatest danger lies in our being unaware of our feelings. If we are aware of our feelings, we are capable of handling them.

Love and displeasure can coexist. The latter does not have to impinge on the former. No one likes to be awakened several times during the night, yet the displeasure at being awakened by her infant does not decrease the mother's love. My mother's sleep was interrupted many times by her twin infants, and I recall her saying, "How wonderful it will be when they sleep through their 2 a.m. feeding." She did not love them any less, and was not threatened by her awareness that their 2 a.m. feeding was an imposition on her comfort.

There is a difference between parents' love for their children and children's love for their parents. Parental love is biological. Animals, too, care tenderly for their young. There is no biological love for parents. Rather it is a love emanating from gratitude and reverence.

It is natural for parents to look after their children. It all began with Adam and Eve, who cared for their children, but did not have any parents to care for. This is how it has remained throughout the ages. There is a popular aphorism, "When a parent leads a child, both are happy. When a child leads a parent, both are unhappy."

> A daughter described her "sandwich role," caring for her 80-year-old mother and her 3-year-old daughter. One can feel the woman's pain as she writes, "I remember being delighted when my daughter decided to toilet train herself. It was the same week my mother became incontinent."
>
> She continues, "When I was growing up, our roles were always very clear. Her job was to critique, guide and teach, and mine was to absorb, react and learn. But now it's as if we've traded parts, like actors in a play who've switched roles on a whim."
>
> It is especially distressing to see a parent become child-like. The woman describes how she makes clownfaced pancakes for both her mother and little girl.
>
> "Between my daughter's ear infections and my mother's occasional falls, the emergency room feels like our second home. ... Going out for an evening is nearly impossible, since few baby-sitters are willing to look after two generations...
>
> "When I'm truly on the brink of despair, something always saves me. My daughter will crawl up in my lap or sing me a little song. My mother, for her part, can surprise me. The other day she told me she is happy now, despite her pain and confusion" (Newsweek, March 4, 2002 p.12).

Parents are not threatened by the feeling that caring for their children can be an imposition. They love their children and this feeling does not generate any guilt. It is different when children's caring for their elderly parents is an imposition. Some children feel guilty for harboring such feelings. "I must be a terrible person to feel that my parents are a burden to me." This may be misinterpreted as a lack of love for them. Consequently, a person may disown the feeling and banish it from consciousness. R' Shlomo Wolbe was right. Disowned feelings can result in emotional problems.

This discussion was a preamble to the incident I will now relate. As a child, I remember Reb Binyamin, a saintly looking man with a long, flowing white beard. Reb Binyamin was a widower, and lived with his son, Laibel. Laibel's devotion and caring for his father was legendary. My father used to refer to Laibel as the finest example of *kibud av* (respect for a father). He used to smilingly relate that Laibel once said to Reb Binyamin, "Pa, I wouldn't give you away for a million dollars, but I wouldn't give a nickel for another one of you."

My father often quoted Laibel's remark as being a healthy attitude. Laibel loved his father, and was sincerely devoted to him, day and night. But Laibel did not have to delude himself that this was not an imposition. There were many things he was not free to do because he had to attend to his father. He willingly sacrificed his comfort, but he was aware that it was a sacrifice. Had he been threatened by the awareness that this was an imposition, he would have had to disown the feeling and would have been unable to deal with it. Buried in his subconscious, the resentment and guilt would have affected his behavior in a way that would have detracted from the care of his father.

This principle applies to many feelings. The Torah is aware that when a person gives *tzedakah*, he may feel imposed upon and have a resentment toward the recipient. One cannot simply be told, "Do not feel resentment." This is why the Torah explains, "You shall surely give to him (the poor), and let your heart not feel bad when you give to him, for in return for this matter, G-d will bless you in all your deeds and in your every undertaking" (*Deuteronomy* 15:10). In other words, *tzedakah* is not a gift. It is an investment which will bring rich returns. Certainly one does not feel bad making an investment which he knows will increase greatly in value. Without such assurance, one might have fulfilled the mitzvah grudgingly.

Laibel was an unusual person. His quip indicated that his love for his father was not diminished by the imposition. For those who may have difficulty in their feelings for their parents for whom they must care, they should look upon this as a wise investment. "Honor your father and your mother, so that your days will be lengthened" (*Exodus* 20:12).

Chutzpah

C hutzpah is hardly a new phenomenon, but it has never before reached its present intensity.

This should not come as a complete surprise. The Talmud predicted that before the final Redemption, "Chutzpah will increase ... the young will humiliate the elders, a son will insult his father and a daughter will rise up against her mother" (*Sotah* 49b). Adolescent psychiatrists report that the most common diagnosis in their clientele is "Oppositional Defiant Disorder."

The watershed appears to have been in the middle of the last century, generally referred to as "the Sixties." There appears to have been an across-the-board rejection of authority. I can recall the fear we had as children if we were threatened to be sent down to the principal's office. Today the principal lives in fear of the students.

In the past, court orders were rarely disobeyed. Being held in contempt of court was a deterrent to disregarding a court order. Police officers were respected. Today court orders are flagrantly defied and police are on the defensive.

Along with this came a defiance of parental authority. In "the sixties" it was assumed that youth had all the usable wisdom. Anyone over 35 was obsolete and antiquated and their words could be disregarded.

As noted earlier, one cannot totally avoid being influenced by one's environment. The traditional parental respect and deference to parental wishes in the Jewish home that was established by the Ten Commandments has suffered significant erosion.

This was a major triumph for the *yetzer hara.* You will recall that R' Avraham Grodzinsky explained that the primary drive of the *yetzer hara* is to cast off all restrictions so that one may freely do whatever one wishes. The rejection of authority and dispensing with all rules for behavior was exactly what the *yetzer hara* wanted.

I have watched some parents groping desperately to establish their authority in the home, but to no avail. The cultural attitude of permissiveness has empowered young people to "do their own thing." Unfortunately, "their own thing" may be self-destructive. The parents stand by, powerless to do anything short of evicting the child from the home. But how can you evict a 14-year-old boy or girl? Where are they to go? Who will care for them? Yet the law does not empower parents to do anything to thwart the child's self-destructive behavior.

Not only is the defiant child self-destructive, but the parent's impotence is made obvious to the other children, whose desire for complete freedom may override whatever deference they had. What a triumph for the *yetzer hara!*

There is only one solution: *parents must teach deference to authority.* As we know, teaching by lecturing is of little value. Children learn primarily from parental modeling. Parents must demonstrate to their children that they set aside their own will in deference to a higher authority.

This is clearly stated: "Nullify your will before His will, so that He will nullify the will of others before your will" (*Ethics of the Fathers* 2:4). Who are the "others" whose will He will nullify? I believe the Talmud may be referring to our children. If we nullify our will before G-d's will, we can expect that He will help us establish authority over our children, and they will set aside their will in favor of their parents' will.

"But," you may say, "I have nullified my will before G-d's will. I am observant of Torah and obey all the restrictions of Torah. Yet, I have not succeeded in gaining obedience from my children."

I believe we are missing a fine point. Listen to what Rashi says: "A person should not say 'I have no desire to eat pork. Rather, I do desire it, but what can I do? My Heavenly Father has decreed that I shall not eat it'" (*Leviticus* 20:26, *Sifra*).

How many people who are observant of Torah can say this? We have developed such disgust of pork that the odor of it can ruin our appetite. This is equally true of most other prohibitions. People who are observant of Shabbos generally do not have to struggle to avoid violating it. It is indeed fortunate that we have so integrated Torah principles that they have become second nature. But by the same token, we are generally unable to comply with the Talmudic statement cited by Rashi, "I do desire it, but what can I do? I must abide by a higher authority." On the other hand, there may be things we wish to do which are not clearly forbidden. It is not unusual, in these instances, that we seek a halachic *heter* (sanction) for them. We must actually search for opportunities to demonstrate that we comply *against* our own will.

Some suggestions come to mind. We have not developed the same opprobrium for *lashon hara* that we have for pork. We may actually be curious to hear a juicy piece of gossip, and not infrequently we may pass it on. Let us demonstrate for our children that as much as we would like to hear something, we must avoid doing so. Whenever someone begins to say something about others that may be negative, we should say, as courteously as possible, "Please, I would like to hear what you have to say, but it appears to me to be *lashon hara*. Let's change the subject."

You may think that saying this may offend others, who may accuse you of trying to be "holier than thou." Even if so, it is one of the few opportunities we have to show deference to authority.

Children know that *lashon hara* is forbidden. If they hear their father or mother speaking *lashon hara*, their deference to parental authority is undermined.

Another opportunity is refraining from conversation in shul. If your child is with you in shul, and your neighbor wishes to tell you something during *davening*, indicate to him that you do not wish to listen. If your neighbor feels offended, so be it. You have demonstrated to your child that as much as you would like to converse, you are nullifying your will before that of the *Shulchan Aruch (Code of Jewish Law)*.

Given the increased prevalence of parental defiance, we should be on the alert for every opportunity to demonstrate to our children that we are obedient to authority even when it goes against our will.

You may think it is picayune, but if your children see you violating the speed limit, you have lost an excellent opportunity to teach deference to authority. If they say, "Daddy, how come all those cars are passing us? Why don't you go faster?" and you respond, "The speed limit here is 55. I don't violate traffic laws," you have taught deference to authority.

It is not uncommon to look for loopholes, both in halachah and in civil law. If we seek ways in which to circumvent authority, we should realize that our children may do likewise.

We must also be cautious not to undermine authority. *When we undermine the authority of others, we also undermine our own.*

A child may come home from school and complain about the teacher, who gave the class or a child an undue punishment or made an unwise comment. There may be a tendency to exclaim, "That's stupid! I'll go to school tomorrow and give that teacher a piece of my mind!"

Be careful! First of all, the child's report may not be accurate. Even if it is, a better response is, "I don't understand that. I'll ask the teacher to explain it to me." Do not undermine the teacher's authority.

Or, you may come home from shul and report something that the rabbi said in his sermon with which you disagree. You may say to your wife, "The rabbi's speech was off the wall today. He said that ... Can you imagine Rabbi C. saying anything like that? These young rabbis think they know everything!" If you say that, you have just dealt a mortal blow to your expectations of your children's obedience.

You do not have to agree with what the rabbi said. There is room for a dissenting opinion. But do not undermine the authority of the rabbi by speaking disrespectfully of him.

Observe the Torah requirements to show respect to the elderly and to honor Torah scholars. If you have parents, remember that how you relate to them will greatly determine how your children react to you.

The *yetzer hara* will do everything in its power to minimize your deference to authority. This makes it so much easier for it to cause your children to be disobedient and defiant.

In addition to deference to authority, Torah demands that every person be shown respect. The Midrash quotes G-d as saying, "My dear children! Is there anything I lack that I must ask it of you? All I do ask of you is that you should love one another and respect one another"(*Tanna D'Vei Eliyahu Rabbah* 28).

Rambam writes, "Do not minimize the importance of respect for others. The sages have permitted some of their restrictive regulations to be set aside to avoid an affront to others' dignity" (*Sanhedrin* 24b).

We observe a mourning period during *Sefirah* (the days of counting the Omer) because during this period thousands of R' Akiva's disciples died in an epidemic. The Talmud says that although they were great Torah scholars, they perished because they were not sufficiently respectful toward each other (*Yevamos* 62b).

The importance of respect for others can be seen from the way our Torah personalities behaved toward everyone.

> *R' Zalman of Vilna stated that all his life he was remorseful for an uncomplimentary remark he had made to someone during a dispute over the interpretation of a passage in Talmud when he was a youth of 14. He soon regretted his words and wished to apologize, but the person had left the study hall. In vain he searched for him throughout Vilna. R' Zalman was unable to shake off his guilt, which continued to plague him.*
>
> *After R' Zalman was married, his father-in-law asked him why he was so dejected, and R' Zalman told him of the incident where he had once humiliated someone. In an effort to relieve R' Zalman's agony, the father-in-law engaged some-one to present himself as if he were the offended person.*
>
> *One day this man came into the study hall and said, "Shalom, R' Zalman. What a long time it has been since we last met!"*
>
> *"I'm sorry, but I don't recall meeting you," R' Zalman said.*
>
> *"Of course you do," the man said. "Don't you remember how we once had a disagreement on a particular passage of the Talmud?"*
>
> *At first, R' Zalman was delighted that he would have the opportunity to ask forgiveness for having offended*

him, but he soon realized that this was not the person, and he understood that this had been a set-up to relieve his guilt. R' Zalman continued to be deep in remorse.

Eventually, word of R' Zalman's anguish reached the Gaon of Vilna, who sent for R' Zalman and said to him, "When a person has done everything humanly possible to rectify a mistake but has been unable to achieve forgiveness, G-d comes to his aid.

"You have done everything within your means to make amends to that person, and there is nothing more you can do. You can be certain that G-d has put it into his heart to forgive you wholeheartedly."

It was only R' Zalman's adoration of the Gaon that enabled him to accept these comforting words and finally divest himself of the guilt he had borne for many years.

This anecdote indicates the seriousness that our *tzaddikim* assigned to respecting the dignity of others. Many stories like this underscore this point.

Chutzpah is not an inborn trait. Children learn it from somewhere, to some degree from their friends, but their prime models are their parents. If the home environment is totally free of chutzpah and is one of great respect of the parents for each other and for everyone, young and old, this can outweigh the negative influence of the chutzpah that they may observe outside the home.

Although I stated that the watershed appears to have been "the Sixties," there was a prophetic insight by R' Klonimus of Piasezna in his work *Chovas HaTalmidim* (R' Klonimus was killed in the Warsaw Ghetto). R' Klonimus states that the defiance of authority is the fulfillment of the Talmudic prediction that chutzpah will thrive.

R' Klonimus adds that today's youth are prematurely independent and have a false maturity of ideas and emotions. They, therefore, see *every* authority figure as a dictator who wishes to control them and deprive them of the pleasures of life.

R' Klonimus suggests that the approach to discipline be with the child's participation. *Chovas HaTalmidim* should be mandatory reading for every parent and teacher.

It is of interest that although G-d controls everything in the universe, He excluded people's ethical and moral behavior from His control. In these areas, we have *bechirah* (free choice). Rather than complying with the Torah teachings simply out of fear, we should come to the realization that we should observe these teachings because they are right and good for us. This constitutes an internal discipline.

Just as we are to emulate all the Divine attributes, we should also emulate His model for following the teachings of elders: internal discipline. In *Chovas HaTalmidim,* R' Klonimus tells us how this can be accomplished.

The Bridge to Nowhere

I was called to the emergency room to see a young man who was asking for help. I introduced myself to this lad of 15 and asked him what his problem was. He remained silent, and my efforts to elicit any information were futile. Eventually he spoke up. "I am a nothing," he said.

"Why do you say you are a nothing?" I asked.

"Well, what am I?" he said. "I'm not a child, and I'm not an adult. I'm a nothing."

It had never occurred to me before this to reflect on the phenomenon of "adolescence." I realize now how wise the Torah was in delineating two phases in life: childhood and adulthood. These are physiological facts. The concept of adolescence is an artifact that was introduced somewhere along the line by Western civilization, and it is an unfortunate concept. Leave it to the *yetzer hara* to take full advantage of Western civilization's error.

In Torah, parents are responsible for a minor child's actions. The moment the boy reaches the end of the last day of his 12th year, and the moment a girl reaches the last instant of her 11th year, they are *immediately* transformed into adults, fully responsible for their actions. A crime committed by a 13-year-old boy is dealt with identically to that committed by a 40-year-old man. *There is no gap in responsibility.*

We live in a culture governed by civil laws which acknowledge a phase of adolescence. We are unable to apply Torah law to youngsters. Once a child reaches adolescence, his parents cannot exert any legal control, other than having the youngster made a ward of the state. Yet, an adolescent is not held fully responsible for his actions because "he has not yet matured." Who, then, is held responsible for his actions? No one.

If a youngster behaves properly, there is of course no problem. But if he deviates, there is little that parents can do other than plead and agonize. If he uses drugs and upsets the entire family, he cannot be forced into treatment. But neither can the parents enforce the rule that the home is a drug-free zone. They cannot legally put a 15-year-old boy or girl into the street. The adolescent knows this and realizes that he or she rather than the parents are in a position of control. The *yetzer hara* seizes this opportunity to entice adolescents to do whatever they wish because the parents are helpless to do anything about it.

Adolescents are aware of the immunity society has given them, and those who are not emotionally healthy may exercise this "privilege" to their own detriment. This is the *yetzer hara's* triumph. It encourages people to do whatever they wish and suffer the consequences.

There is an additional complication resulting from adolescence. *Once a person has experienced the freedom from responsibility, this may leave its mark on him.* In other words, even when a person fully "matures" and is a legally responsible adult, the experience of having at one time been free of responsibility may impact upon his adult behavior. Some adults do things that they know are wrong just to see if they "can get away with it." This is often a by-product of adolescence.

We must combat this destructive *yetzer hara* in every way possible. We should make "bar-mitzvah" and "bas-mitzvah" meaningful occasions rather than just parties. Too often, the ceremony in the synagogue and the subsequent celebration fails to impress the young boy with the solemnity of the occasion. Of course the occasion should be a joyous one, but it should be more than having a good time and receiving gifts.

Parents should discuss with their children the full meaning of the blessing thanking G-d "Who has freed me from the punishment due this child." For a boy, this is said when he is called to the Torah. For a girl, it may be said when the family gathers at home for celebration of her 12th birthday. The children should be told that in the eyes of G-d they are adults, fully accountable for their actions, and that is why the father thanks G-d that he was privileged to raise them to the age of accountability.

Parents should become knowledgeable of the concept of *kabbalas ol* (accepting the yoke of Torah), and discuss with their children the centrality of this concept in Judaism. The children should be helped to understand that until their bar- or bas-mitzvah age, they were reciting the *Shema* as *chinuch* (training), but that now it is for real. Their obligation to fast on Yom Kippur is no less than that of adults.

In some families, girls begin lighting the Shabbos candles at age 12. As important as family tradition is, I personally feel that the conditions of modern society warrant consideration of beginning this practice in families where this has not been the custom. If the mother bakes the *challah* for Shabbos, a girl of 12 should be given the mitzvah of separating the portion of dough known as *challah* and reciting the *berachah*. Boys, of course, have the mitzvah of *tefillin*. When a *mezuzah* is affixed to the doorpost, allowing the girl over 12 or the boy over 13 to do this helps impress upon them that they have indeed entered the age of mitzvos.

We may not be able to change society, but if we treat our children of mitzvah age as adults and expect responsible behavior from them, they are likely to think of themselves as adults. This can help counter the *yetzer hara's* nefarious attack on our children.

Pursuit of Truth

Among the predictions in the Mishnah in *Sotah* cited above is that in the generation before the Redemption, "truth will be absent."

One might ask: Why will truth be absent? Even if not everyone will be perfectly truthful, certainly some truth will exist. It is inconceivable that the entire world population will constantly be lying.

The answer is that truth is more than just not lying. Not lying is a negative quality. Truth is a positive quality.

The correct definition of truth is not simple. Two contemporary ethicists, R' Eliyahu Dessler and R' Shlomo Wolbe, have grappled with it. The editor of *Michtav M'Eliyahu* states that R' Dessler devoted much time and effort toward clarifying the essence of truth.

R' Dessler points out that if someone weighs diamonds, where an infinitesimally small error can be extremely costly, one makes certain that the balance scale is functioning with absolute accuracy. The slightest defect in the accuracy of the scale is intolerable.

We make important decisions every day that affect the lives of others as well as our own. These are based on judgments we make, some with greater deliberation, some with less and some almost automatically. Every judgment requires consideration of a variety of factors and weighing the pros and cons for each. The "balance scale" we use is our mind. How accurate is this scale? Most often there are already some items on the scale that may distort the balance in favor of one side. If so, we are not giving a "true weight." If a merchant used a scale that was slanted in his favor, that would constitute fraud. It is no less fraudulent when we use a biased scale for our judgments.

R' Dessler gives an excellent example. A person wishes to know whether it is permissible to play chess on Shabbos, and consults the *Shulchan Aruch* (Code of Jewish Law). Obviously, he desires to play chess. He cannot approach the *Shulchan Aruch* objectively. Unless the halachah is printed in unequivocal bold, large letters, he will look for those rulings that will allow him to do what he desires.

R' Dessler says that we generally have biases when weighing a decision. We wish the decision to be one that will be most comfortable. Our judgment scale is slanted and does not give a true weight. (*Michtav M'Eliyahu*, vol. 1, *Mabat Ha'Emes*).

In addition to distortion by desire, judgments can also be distorted by prejudice (pre-judice); i.e., by an opinion one holds before one considers all the facts. R' Chaim Shmulevitz cites the halachah that a *dayan* (magistrate) may not listen to one litigant in the absence of the other. Even though he knows that he must yet listen to an opposing argument and that he should not yet come to any conclusion, he is likely to form an opinion based on what he heard first, and he can no longer be objective. R' Chaim says that this is the logic behind "sin begets sin." To avoid repetition of the sin, one must admit that what he did was wrong. It takes great courage to relinquish a belief. The reluctance to recognize that one did wrong distorts one's perception and judgment and can lead to further sin (*Sichos Mussar* 5732:21).

The observation by these ethicists has been confirmed. Not infrequently, scientific and medical research has been found to be flawed because the researchers did not report findings that conflicted with their theories. These were not necessarily willful concealments. Just as often, contradictory findings were simply overlooked. Just as a bribe blinds the perception of a judge so that he may not be able to see what is before him (*Deuteronomy* 16:19), so may the desire to prove one's theory blind a researcher to findings that tend to disprove it.

The overriding importance of truth is pointed out by R' Chaim Shmulevitz. He cites the Torah account of Moses reprimanding Aaron for not eating the sacrificial offering on the day his two sons died, because G-d had commanded that they eat it. Aaron suggested that perhaps Moses had misunderstood the Divine commandment, whereupon Moses responded, "You are correct. I did not remember what G-d told me" (*Leviticus* 10:20, *Rashi,* in some editions).

R' Chaim says that Moses was in a dilemma. How could he admit that he had mistaken the Divine command? Inasmuch as he was the only conduit for G-d's commandments, admitting that he had forgotten or misinterpreted G-d's word would put the entire Torah in doubt forever. People might say, "If Moses was capable of a mistake about this particular command, how can we be certain that he was not mistaken about others?" Perhaps he should say to Aaron, "Do as I said. That is G-d's wish."

However, R' Chaim says, Moses decided, "I cannot deviate from the truth. If that will cast doubt on the authenticity of the Torah, then it will be up to G-d to set that straight. It is not my duty to preserve the Torah for eternity. My duty is to be truthful, regardless of what the fallout may be."

Inasmuch as we all have desires, how can we ever make a truly objective judgment? R' Dessler suggests that we do our utmost to refine our *middos*, which will lessen the tendency to err. He suggests that any decision which is made without conscious deliberation and considering all factors should be suspect. This will not guarantee objectivity, but will lessen the degree of distortion. Finally, recognizing our vulnerability to err due to bias, we should consult competent Torah scholars for advice.

R' Wolbe adds another important principle. The only absolute truth in the universe is G-d. "G-d is truth" (*Jeremiah* 10:10). The closer we come to G-d, the closer we are to truth.

The Torah says that we are to cleave unto G-d (*Deuteronomy* 30:20). The Talmud states that this can be accomplished by emulating the Divine attributes of mercy and kindness. The more we identify with G-d, the more truthful we become. This explains R' Dessler's statement that refinement of *middos* leads to truth.

The Midrash states that before G-d created man He held counsel with the angels. The Angel of Truth said that man should not be created because "he is wholly falsehood." G-d threw the Angel of Truth down to earth.

The meaning of this Midrash is that man, as a physical being, cannot possibly be truthful, because his thinking is influenced by his many physical desires. Placing the Angel of Truth on earth means that G-d gave the Torah to us earthlings, as we say in the *berachah* for reading of the Torah, "He gave us a Torah of truth." Physical man without Torah is incapable of truth. Torah enables a person to achieve truth, if he pursues it with great diligence.

Pursuit of truth requires open-mindedness. The Talmud states that the reason that halachah was established by the opinion of the school of Hillel was not only because they were less stringent but also because they always quoted the opinion of the opposing school of Shammai before stating their own opinion (*Eruvin* 13b). This open-mindedness and willingness to consider a dissenting view gave greater validity to their position.

R' Yechezkel Levenstein cites the verse (*Exodus* 18:1) that Jethro came to the Israelite encampment in the desert because he heard of the miraculous escape of the Jews and their triumph over the Egyptians. R' Levenstein notes that others had also heard of this (*Exodus* 15:14-15), yet none of them were motivated to come to the Israelites. He says that the reason Jethro was impressed by what he heard was because he had researched all existing religions and found them to be without substance (*Rashi, Exodus* 18:11). His mind was open to hear about the miracles of the G-d of Israel. Other nations heard as well, but because they were devoted to their pagan beliefs, they were closed minded and refractory to the evidence of even supernatural miracles.

Even the most striking evidence and irrefutable arguments will not impress anyone whose mind is closed. Pursuit of truth requires a willingness to listen to opinions other than one's own.

Pursuit of truth also means to pursue absolute honesty with oneself. R' Chaim of Sanz, when reciting the thirteen principles of faith following morning services, would say, "I believe with perfect faith ... No, Chaim, you are not telling the truth." He would meditate a while and again say, "I believe with perfect faith ... Chaim, you are still not telling the truth." This would continue until he felt he had achieved complete belief.

Perhaps we cannot reach the spiritual heights of our great Torah luminaries, but it is inspiring to know the level which a human being is capable of reaching.

> *R' Eliyahu David Rabinowiz-Tumim, who was known as the Aderes, had a daughter who died in her youth. The Chevrah Kadisha (burial organization) knew how punctual the Aderes was, and they were ready to begin*

the funeral at the appointed time. Much to their surprise, the Aderes did not come out of his study for a while.

When the Aderes emerged, he apologized for the delay and explained, "I must recite the berachah (blessing) Baruch Dayan Ha'Emes (Blessed [is G-d,] the truthful Judge). The Talmud requires that one recite this berachah with the same spirit that one would praise G-d for good happenings. I realized that I was unable to do so. I had to meditate and recall all the mussar teachings I had heard, until I was able to reach the trust in G-d's judgment that everything He does is for the good."

As I commented about the Chafetz Chaim, it is this degree of spirituality that brings G-d to say to the heavenly angels, "See the masterful creature I created."

Torah Is Timeless

The *yetzer hara* may try to convince people that some Torah laws are obsolete. Whereas they were necessary in ancient times, it will say, things are so different today that these laws are no longer relevant. This argument may appear logical, but we must remember that Torah is Divine and timeless.

This argument is that of the *ben rasha*, the wicked son in the Haggadah. His question, "Of what purpose is this service (the offering of the Passover sacrifice) to you?" is not a negation of the original mitzvah. He admits that inasmuch as the lamb was the Egyptian totem, sacrificing the lamb was a sign of liberation from Egyptian rule and a repudiation of idolatry. Granted, this was appropriate at the time of the Exodus, but is irrelevant now. Paganism is long gone, and there is no need to repudiate idolatry.

The answer in the Haggadah is that he is dishonest. Had he lived at the time of the Exodus, he would have found other reasons to disobey. He would not have repudiated idolatry then, and does not repudiate idolatry even today.

As we noted earlier, Jews were never so foolish as to believe that idols were gods. Rather, they sought to have a god whom they could create and to whom they could dictate what laws to make. This would allow them to eliminate any laws that interfered with their self-gratification. Anyone who tampers with Torah laws in order to eliminate restrictions that inconvenience him is essentially practicing idolatry, even if he does not worship an icon.

> Two litigants came before a beis din (rabbinic tribunal). One claimed that he had ordered merchandise from the other to be delivered on a specific day. The merchandise did not arrive until much later, which caused him a significant loss. After listening to both sides, the rabbi ruled that the provider had to compensate the merchant for his loss.
>
> The other litigant objected, but the rabbi said, "I'm sorry, but that is the ruling according to Torah law."
>
> "When was the Torah given?" the provider asked.
>
> "It was given on the sixth day of Sivan," the rabbi answered.
>
> "There you have it," the losing litigant exclaimed. "In Sivan the weather is dry and the roads are passable. That's why the Torah considers failure to deliver to be a dereliction. But if the Torah had been given during the winter, when the roads are muddy or snow covered, the Torah would have ruled otherwise."

Assigning Torah to any period in history is a denial of its Divine origin. It is the Divine wisdom, and is as eternal as G-d. Any argument that Torah is obsolete is nothing other than the *yetzer hara's* attempt to be free of all restrictions.

Harmony in the Home

Among the dire predictions in the Talmud (*Sotah* 49b) is that "a person's foes will be the members of his own household." The increase in family disruptions in the past several decades is the tragic fulfillment of the Talmudic prophesy.

That disrupting families is a goal of the *yetzer hara* is evident from the Talmudic story of a couple who would get into an argument every Shabbos eve. R' Meir stayed with them for three Shabbos evenings and restored their *shalom bayis*. The voice of Satan was then heard saying, "Woe! R' Meir has expelled me from this home" (*Gittin* 52a). The recent increase in domestic dissent is thus the work of the *yetzer hara,* which has intensified its assault against *shalom bayis*. This requires a corresponding increase in our defenses against this attack.

The strongest defense against the *yetzer hara* is a relationship of true love and devotion. As noted, we are not immune to the ideas that prevail in our environment. The runaway rate of failed marriages in the secular world seems to have impacted the Jewish community, with the number of divorces being at an unprecedented high.

The vulnerability of environmental influence which Rambam cites is best illustrated by a story about R' Moshe Sofer (Chasam Sofer). If he was consulted by a person whose *middos* were unrefined, he would follow the conversation by studying *mussar*. He told his students that simply being in the presence of a person with coarse *middos* can have a negative impact!

The hedonistic attitude of Western civilization has affected the family as well. It is only natural to desire gratification in a relationship. But if the principal basis of a marriage is self-gratification, the marriage is vulnerable to turbulence.

The Torah concept of the marriage relationship is, "A man must love his wife as much as he loves himself, and must respect her even more than he respects himself" (*Yevamos* 62b). Halachah requires mutual consideration and respect (*Rambam, Hil. Ishus* 15:19-20).

Let us not delude ourselves that we have not been affected by the secular concepts of love and marriage, which are essentially comprised of self-gratification. Rambam's statement (*Hil. Dei'os* 6:1) that a person is profoundly affected by his environment is undeniable.

Self-love is a fact of nature. Love of another person has to be learned, and it takes much effort to bring love of another person to the level of love of oneself, which the Torah requires in marriage. The love of another that is so common in our environment is often nothing but self-love.

> *The Rebbe of Kotzk noticed a young man thoroughly enjoying a dish of fish. "Why are you eating fish?" the Rebbe asked.*
>
> *The young man responded, "Why? Because I love fish, that's why."*
>
> *"So it was your love for the fish that caused you to take it from the water, kill it and cook it! If you really loved the fish, you would have let it live. Do not delude yourself, young man. What you really love is yourself, and because the fish satisfies your palate, you eat it."*

The spontaneous bond that occurs between man and woman generally begins as self-love, but if it remains at this level, the relationship is on very shaky ground. Whenever one's needs are not met by the other, the primary basis of the relationship is weakened and strife may occur. It is incumbent that husband and wife make the effort to proceed beyond self-love and develop a love for the other that is at least equal to the love of oneself. Add to this the Talmudic requirement that a husband's respect for his wife should exceed that which he expects for himself, and you will have created a bond in marriage that can withstand any stress.

Rambam is very explicit in forbidding verbal abuse (*Hil. Ishus* 15:19). One cannot claim to be observant of Torah if one violates this halachah any more than if one violates any other halachah. Just as eating meat with milk together is prohibited, so is shouting at one's spouse or using insulting language prohibited.

R' Avraham Pam says that antagonizing one's wife is a Scriptural transgression. The Torah says, "You shall not aggrieve your fellow" (*Leviticus* 25:17). The Chinuch says, "A child who is aggrieved complains to his father. A woman who is aggrieved complains to her husband" (*Sefer HaChinuch, Mitzvah* 65). If a husband aggrieves his wife, her agony is severe, because she has no one to turn to. The Talmud says that a husband should take great care not to aggrieve his wife, because women are emotionally more sensitive (*Bava Metzia* 59b).

The Talmud says that an honored person is one who honors others (*Ethics of the Fathers* 4:1). An honorable husband is one who honors his wife (*Atarah LaMelech* p. 35).

The *yetzer hara* appears to have been effective in allowing people who are ritually observant but who are abusive in the home to think that they are compliant with Torah. Judaism rejects any dichotomy in behavior. The notion of keeping G-d out of our everyday affairs is antithetical to Judaism. Torah requires, "Know G-d in *all* your ways" (*Proverbs* 3:6). Indeed, the Talmud cites this verse as *the principle upon which all of*

Torah is dependent (*Berachos* 63a). We must combat the assault of the *yetzer hara* on family life by strengthening our resolve to know G-d in *all* that we do. How we relate to members of our household is governed by halachah no less than is observance of Shabbos.

A young man consulted the Steipler Gaon for guidance on how to schedule his learning, and the Gaon gave him precise instructions. Just as the young man was about to walk out the door, the Gaon called him back.

> *"I see that you are very devoted to Torah study,"* he said, *"but you must remember to help out at home."*
>
> *The young man was taken aback. "My wife is very G-d fearing, and it is her fervent wish that I dedicate myself wholly to learning," he said.*
>
> *"That is indeed her mitzvah,"* the Gaon said, *"but your mitzvah is to help with the housework. When you come home for lunch, you must ask her what there is that you can do to help."* The Gaon paused a moment, then repeated, *"The very first thing on coming home is to ask how you can be of help."*

You will recall R' Elchanan Wasserman's comment that if it is to its advantage, the *yetzer hara* will push a person to do "mitzvos"; i.e, what *it* considers to be a mitzvah. How careful we must be to avoid this dangerous pitfall!

R' Avraham Pam says, "*Gemilas chasadim* (acts of kind-ness) is indeed a very great mitzvah, but not at the expense of others.

"Suppose," R' Pam says, "that a husband usually comes home for dinner at 6 o'clock. His wife has made an extra effort to prepare his favorite dish, and she looks forward to his being home at 6 o'clock. But it is 6:15, 6:30, 7 o'clock, and no sign of her husband. What has happened to him? What should she do with the dinner? This dish loses its taste if it is reheated.

"At 7:45 the husband comes in. A friend had to catch a plane and he drove him to the airport.

"How sad, how sad," says R' Pam, "that he did not consider that his wife's anguish might outweigh the merit of the *chessed* to his friend" (*Atarah LaMelech* p. 125).

R' Pam continues, "When the Israelites in the desert complained to Moses that they were bored with the manna, G-d said, 'The manna is so special. Just look what My children are complaining about!' (*Rashi, Numbers* 11:6).

"A husband returns home from work and finds toys strewn all over the living room. He complains to his wife why she lets the house become so messy. At this point, G-d says, 'Look what My children are complaining about!' How many couples cry for a child? How many go through difficult procedures in the hope of having a child, and suffer deep disappointment? If only they could be fortunate enough to have toys strewn all over the house! A bit of gratitude and consideration would avoid a spat with his wife" (*Atarah LaMelech* p. 128).

The first attack of Amalek was against the weakest of Israel (*Deuteronomy* 25:18), and the *yetzer hara* continues this stratagem. The *yetzer hara* cunningly exploits people's weaknesses to undermine *shalom bayis*. Some people are power hungry, and take advantage of any situation to exert control over others. When they do this in the home, they may become tyrants. Offending the dignity of a spouse is a frank violation of the Talmudic requirement to "respect a wife *even more* than one respects oneself."

The Talmud is replete with statements about proper attitudes within the home. It is for this reason that the very first *berachah* after husband and wife have been united in marriage is "Blessed is G-d Who created everything for His glory." This is a message to the young couple that the ultimate goal of their marriage is *not* gratification of their individual needs, but to establish a family that will bring greater glory to G-d. If frustrations in a relationship occur, they must be approached within the framework of the Torah concept of marriage. Under such circumstances, differences can be overcome. If the *yetzer hara* succeeds in making gratification of one's wishes the basis for the marriage relationship, differences strike at the very core of the marriage.

Shalom bayis is the strength of Jewish survival. *Shalom bayis* does not mean that husband and wife must always be of the same opinion. R' Shlomo Wolbe states that *darkei shalom* (ways of peace) does not mean unanimity of opinion. Rather, it means building a bridge and creating harmony between two conflicting opinions. "*Shalom bayis* does not mean absence of differences. The latter means only that the couple have not reached closeness of their minds. *Shalom bayis* means that their differences are evident, but that they succeeded in bridging them" (*Alei Shur* vol. 1 p. 257.).

Of course there can be differences of opinion between a couple, but they must learn to disagree with respect and harmonize their differences.

The *yetzer hara* seeks opportunities to cause the most harm. If it succeeds in disrupting a marriage, it has not only devastated two individuals, but has inflicted enduring harm on the children. Yes, children may ultimately make an adjustment to the tension within the family, but it comes at great cost to them. Destroying *shalom bayis* is, therefore, a major triumph for the *yetzer hara.*

We must wrest ourselves free from the insidious influences of our environment and return to the Torah concept of marriage. We cannot relax our efforts to resist the *yetzer hara.*

In the historic battle against Amalek, we were victorious only as long as Moses' arms were raised in prayer. When he relaxed his arms, Amalek triumphed. Because it was difficult for Moses to keep his arms elevated, Aaron and Chur supported them (*Exodus* 17:12). We must seek every source of support to elevate ourselves and maintain the edge over the *yetzer hara.* Repeated and sincere study and implementation of the teachings of *mussar* in order to refine our *middos* is essential if we are to triumph in this crucial struggle.

Prayer

As we noted, the victory in the battle with Amalek was contingent upon Moses' prayer. On the verse "The voice is the voice of Jacob, but the hands are the hands of Esau" (*Genesis* 27:22), the Midrash says, "As long as the voice of Jacob is heard in prayer, the hands and might of Esau are powerless" (*Bereishis Rabbah* 65:16). Knowing that prayer is our most powerful weapon, the *yetzer hara* has made a frontal assault on it.

The Talmud says that *tefillah* is superior even to performance of mitzvos (*Berachos* 32 b). With all the reassurances we are given about the potency of *tefillah*, we may ask: Why does it appear that our prayers are so often unanswered?

The answer to this was given by R' Yom Tov Heller, author of *Tosafos Yom Tov*. Following the horrific pogroms of 1648 in which entire Jewish communities were destroyed, the *Tosafos Yom Tov* said that this occurred because Jews desecrated prayer by conversing in shul. Although unfortunately there were Jews who were not observant of Shabbos and kashrus, the *Tosafos Yom Tov* did not incriminate them as responsible for the calamity. Ironically, it was those Jews who *were* observant of Torah and did attend *shul* that he claimed were at fault.

The *yetzer hara* knows that telling a Torah-observant person to eat *tereifah* is futile. It, therefore, chooses to advise him to commit sins which one does not take seriously, such as irreverence in a shul.

> R' Yosef Chaim Sonnenfeld never opened or closed a window because of heat or cold in the shul without asking permission from the shammes (beadle). He explained, "If I were to be in the palace of a king, would I have the audacity to open or close the windows? The shul is G-d's palace, and must be respected as such."
>
> One time after services, a person came into the shul and asked R' Yosef Chaim for advice. While R' Yosef Chaim was talking to him, someone came into the shul, and upon noticing them exclaimed, "Carrying on conversation in the shul!" R' Yosef Chaim promptly escorted the consultee into the hallway and continued the conversation there. After that, R' Yosef Chaim never spoke anything but prayer and words of Torah in the shul, and said he was grateful for the rebuke.

In one shul, after the rabbi delivered a sermon denouncing conversation in shul, one congregant said, "What does he want from us? For me the shul is a social club." How tragic that some people have lost reverence for the shul as a house of G-d!

It is one thing if someone avoids an opportunity to have an audience with the king. However, if one is privileged to be in the king's presence, and while the king is listening to him one turns away to carry on a conversation with someone else, this is an unforgivable affront.

How painful it is to see that the rabbi must stop the *chazzan* (reader) multiple times during the services to restore quiet in the shul. Repeated pleas to curtail conversation during *davening* fall on deaf ears. This can only be the result of the unrelenting work of the *yetzer hara* to neutralize our most potent weapon of prayer.

Lack of *kavannah* (concentration) in prayer is not a new phenomenon. Two thousand years ago the Talmud stated, "If one makes his prayer routine, it is not a supplication" (*Berachos* 28b). There were always distractions in prayer. However, the more complex our lives become, the more issues we deal with, the more likely our minds are to drift.

Unfortunately, *davening* as if one were running a race is not a new phenomenon. But this, too, has further deteriorated in recent times.

One of the side effects of the technological revolution is that we have lost our tolerance for delay. Speed has acquired value of its own, and the prevailing ethos is the faster the better. We are the beneficiaries of jet planes, even super-sonic flight, microwave ovens, fax machines and computers that can do thousands of calculations in the fraction of a second. Our kitchen cupboards contain many "instant" food products that are inferior in taste. Fast-food vendors are thriving even though home-cooked food is much healthier. Copier salespeople can easily convince businesses to replace their "obsolete" copiers that can make only sixty copies a minute with a "state-of-the-art" model that can put out one hundred fifty copies a minute. A bit of rational thinking would reveal that the extra expenditure will not really improve the bottom line at all, but emotions outweigh reason: the faster the better.

This impatience often manifests itself in our prayers. True, we must often begin our workday early, but is a five- or ten-minute difference really so crucial? Yet, there are many shuls that finish the morning service in twenty-five minutes. One can hardly have much *kavannah* when one races through the prayers at such high speed.

Here, too, we must combat the modern *yetzer hara*. We may do so by simply making a serious resolve that we will remain in shul for no less than forty-five minutes, regardless of how soon one finishes the morning prayers. The additional twenty minutes will not impoverish anyone. If we allow this additional time for prayer and make a concerted effort at *kavannah,* we can rescue this most important component of life from its deteriorated state.

There are important readings about *tefillah* in the Shulchan Aruch and in the writings of *chassidus* and *mussar.* If we studied these, we would realize the great significance of *tefillah* and make an extra effort to increase the quality of our prayers.

The Control Issue

"**E**verything is in the hands of G-d except the fear of
G-d" (*Berachos* 33b). This a fundamental principle
of Judaism. The only freedom of choice one has
(*bechirah*) is in choosing between right and wrong. Ethical
and moral behavior are the only prerogatives of humans.
Everything else is determined by G-d.

A person may think that one can control one's destiny. The
story of Joseph and his brothers teaches us otherwise. The
Midrash states that when the brothers sought to foil the
predictions of Joseph's dreams, G-d said, "We shall see
whose will shall be carried out, Mine or theirs" (*Rashi, Exodus*
27:20). Indeed, the very act whereby the brothers sought to
thwart Joseph's becoming their master was the one which
brought about his elevation to the position of second to the
king of Egypt.

Is it not ironic that we spend the lion's share of our lives on
things beyond our control, while ignoring those things where
our choices can make a difference?

How much we think we can control is often affected by our
life style. For example, in the treatment of alcoholism, the

most difficult obstacle to recovery is the alcoholic's refusal to accept that he does not have control over his drinking. The resistance to accepting loss of control is particularly severe in those people who exert control in other areas of their lives. This is why high achievers such as doctors, executives, lawyers and other professionals who wield a measure of control over other people's lives have great difficulty in accepting that they do not have control over their drinking.

Among the many thousands of alcoholics I have treated, the most resistant patient I can recall was a baseball pitcher whose fastball is legendary. He pitched his team to three World Series championships because he was able to throw a ball at over one hundred miles per hour and direct it within millimeters of its target. With such incomparable control over a baseball it was virtually impossible for him to realize that he had no control whatsoever over alcohol.

In the past, it was much easier for people to accept the limitation of their control. After all, how much control did they have? If you drove a horse-driven wagon and wanted the horse to turn left, you pulled the left rein. This did not actually *control* the horse, but by causing the horse to feel pain, the horse turned to the left to relieve the pain. The choice was actually the horse's. If the horse saw a pile of hay to its right and the discomfort of its hunger exceeded the discomfort of the bit, it could defy the driver and choose to turn to the right.

Driving an automobile is much different. When you turn the steering wheel, you are not giving the car a choice. You are exerting actual and complete control.

The automobile is hardly the only thing we control. In the past, one had to make a fire to heat the home, and there was nothing one could do for relief from torrid heat. Today, with the touch of a finger we change the climate within our home to our liking. We can also wield control over our home appliances from our workplace via telephone. We can turn on the air conditioner and oven from a distance, so that the house will be cool and the roast done when we arrive home.

Much of our workday may be spent pressing buttons to exert electronic controls. As a child, I had a toy car which I had to push along the floor. The other day I saw a 3-year-old child gleefully controlling the movements of a toy truck across the room via a remote electronic control. I actually felt a chill when the Mission Control was able to control Explorer II when it was beyond the solar system, over *two billion miles from earth.* How can we relinquish the illusion of control when we can control things in outer space?

Genetic manipulation has opened up a new vista of control. In the not-too-distant future, parents will be able to control the gender, hair color, and color of the eyes of a fetus. Some control has already been wielded over plants and the end is nowhere in sight.

Make no mistake. Our great scientific and technological advances are giving us unprecedented control over many things. However, the more we feel we can control some things, the more we feel that we should be able to control *everything*: our future, our spouses, our children and even our friends.

Moses warned the Israelites that when they inherit the Promised Land, "You may say in your heart, 'My strength and the might of my hand made me all this wealth.' Then you shall remember that it was G-d Who gave you the strength to make wealth" (*Deuteronomy* 8:17-18). It is so easy to delude ourselves that what we achieve is totally the result of our own effort.

Believing that we can control things is especially dangerous when we try to exert control over other people. Many family problems are the result of control. The attempt to control a spouse often results in emotional or physical abuse. The attempt to control one's children often results in defiance.

There is nothing the *yetzer hara* wishes to do more than to cause discord within families. As we noted, the primary drive of the *yetzer hara* is to be free of all restrictions. The desire of a spouse or parent to control the other spouse or children is diametrically opposed to the desire of the others to be free. This provides the most fertile ground for development of opposition and dissent.

Spouses should respect each other's will, and true, unselfish love will result in each wishing to give happiness to the other. This will eliminate any need for authoritarian control.

My father never shouted at me, and never physically disciplined me. However, the thought that I would do anything that would displease him never occurred to me because of my great respect for him. It was a respect that he had earned.

Parents' love for their children is biologic. Children's love for their parents must be acquired. The dependence of children on their parents may produce resentment. When parents conduct themselves in a manner that earns their children's admiration and respect, this overrides the resentment. Obedience of parents should be the result of reverence and appreciation, not of control.

The need to control others and "show them who's boss" is often the result of a person trying to gain stature by dominating others. Exerting control is indicative of low self-esteem.

In my other books I have repeatedly stressed the importance of self-esteem. Spouses or parents with good self-esteem know that they can be loved, appreciated and respected. They have no need to be authoritarian.

As we have seen, the *yetzer hara* tries to crush a person and make one feel inadequate and unworthy. The ingredients of low-self esteem, the need to control and the inherent resistance to being dominated make up a perfect recipe for discord and unhappiness, giving the *yetzer hara* its greatest triumph.

Judgment in Depression

Statistics indicate that an unprecedented number of people are suffering from clinical depression. It is possible that this reflects a greater awareness rather than an actual increase, but my forty years of psychiatric practice lead me to believe that there is indeed an actual increase in the number of people suffering from depression as well as a greater awareness. The reason for this increase is not known. The history of psychiatry shows that in different eras, different psychiatric disorders prevailed.

In *Getting Up When You're Down* I discussed the different varieties of depressive disorders. My purpose here is to show how the *yetzer hara* may exploit these conditions for its destructive goal.

R' Chaim Shmulevitz in *Sichos Mussar* cites the episode of the Israelites' worship of the Golden Calf shortly after the Exodus. He notes that just several weeks after they had attained the highest level of spirituality known to mankind, the revelation at Sinai, they abruptly sank to the depths of degeneracy of idolatry. R' Shmulevitz points out that this is not the way the *yetzer hara* usually operates. A person who is meticulously observant of Torah, who has studied Torah since dawn and *davened* with great *kavannah* does not leave shul and run off to McDonalds for a cheeseburger. Deviation from Torah is very gradual and may even be imperceptible, beginning with a very minor infringement and proceeding slowly to more serious violations. How could the Israelites have sustained so precipitous a fall in so short a time?

R' Shmulevitz says that the gradual deviation occurs when a person is emotionally stable. However, if one is in a state of depression, errors in judgment may result in very radical changes.

When Moses did not return at the expected time, Satan deluded the Israelites that Moses had died. Stranded in the arid desert without their trusted leader, the Israelites panicked and fell into a state of depression. In this state of mind, R' Shmulevitz says, normal judgment is suspended and precipitous violations may occur.

This is an extremely important observation. When depressed, a person's perceptions and judgment may be grossly distorted and one is capable of committing most serious blunders. As with any delusion, one is certain that one's perceptions and judgments are correct, and one may reject sound advice.

People in depression have gotten divorced, quit their jobs, broken off relationships with parents and friends, sold their homes, relocated and self-medicated with alcohol or drugs. Of course, none of these relieve the depression. When the depres-sion wears off, one is left with the ruins of one's misjudgments, which is enough reason to be thrust into another depression.

Because of the apparent current increase in clinical de-pression, it is important to be alert that this condition may occur to anyone. However, because many people believe that clinical depression, as a psychiatric illness, is a reflection on one's character, they are reluctant to admit that they may be suffering from it. Instead, they may attribute their misery to any one of many causes, and make unwise decisions in the hope that these will relieve their depression.

Getting Up When You're Down is recommended reading for everyone. It explains that clinical depression is due to a chemical imbalance in the body, and is not due to a weakness of character. It is a medical problem which can and should be appropriately treated. Because of the fear that being treated for depression may somehow become public knowledge and affect the marriage prospects of family members, some people resist acknowledging the condition and accepting treatment. This is most foolish. Failure to treat a clinical depression can have very serious consequences.

Always on the lookout for ways in which it can disable or ruin a person, the *yetzer hara* takes advantage of depression to accomplish its goal. As R' Shmulevitz so aptly points out, it was just such a maneuver of the *yetzer hara* that resulted in our ancestors committing a grave sin (*Numbers* 14:1), the effects of which we are still enduring.

Of the various symptoms of clinical depression, feelings of worthlessness and despair are the most serious. All initiative and interest to do anything may be lost, and one cannot see any light at the end of the tunnel. Little wonder that one may take drastic steps to escape this intense distress.

Do not allow the yetzer hara to victimize you. If feelings of severe dejection and despair occur, seek competent help. Remember that the *yetzer hara* may masquerade as a *tzaddik* and try to convince you how sinful you have been, and that because of your sins G-d has rejected you. It may bring to mind things that happened many years ago and make you think that you have committed unforgivable sins. Be alert to its cunning. Accept the observations and suggestions of family and friends that you are suffering from a treatable condition. Get the necessary help to feel better and to thwart the evil designs of the *yetzer hara*.

The Severest Wound

The Midrash states that before G-d gave the Torah to the Israelites, He asked them, "Who will guarantee that you will observe My Torah?" The Jews answered, "The Patriarchs, Abraham, Isaac and Jacob." G-d did not accept this. "They are of the past," He said. "Our children will be our guarantors," the Jews said. G-d accepted this.

Indeed, as illustrious as our past has been, it provides no assurance that Israel will continue to observe the Torah. The only assurance we have is our children.

How painful it is to see that many of our children are drifting away from Torah. I am not referring to those raised in homes where there was no Torah observance. I am referring to the loss of children from the finest, Torah-observant homes. This phenomenon is alarming, particularly since the problem appears to be escalating.

In its desire to inflict a mortal wound, the *yetzer hara* has directed its attack on our children. We must find ways to combat this greatest of all dangers.

I was called to attend an emergency meeting to discuss the problem of "the hemorrhaging loss of our children."

Attending this meeting were representatives of various yeshivos and chassidic communities. I wish to share with you the comments at this meeting.

One person said, "I'll tell you why the problem is increasing. Years ago there were, say, 10,000 students in the yeshivos. If 1 percent were misfits, then there were about one hundred of these dispersed throughout New York. If anyone left the yeshivah environment, they had nowhere to go. Because they needed to belong somewhere, they remained in the yeshivah. Eventually some of them made a better adjustment and remained within the fold.

"Today there are 100,000 yeshivah students, and the same 1 percent misfits are now a large enough group to form a community, which is exactly what they have done. As a result, any youngster who is having some adjustment problem in the yeshivah now has a community in the street which will welcome him with open arms. Every yeshivah dropout increases the size of that community, which makes it easier for other youngsters to find a group with whom they can associate outside of the yeshivah. This problem can only get worse."

Another person said, "You think that when I was in the yeshivah there were no bums? But I did not want to leave the yeshivah because I did not want to lose the closeness with and respect of my parents.

"Many of today's youngsters are not afraid of losing the closeness to their parents because they feel there is nothing to lose. The father does not have time for his children. He comes home at 8 p.m. from work. He has a cell phone and a beeper on his belt, and is talking to someone on the house phone. If the child approaches him he may say, 'Can't you see I'm busy now? This is an important call.' The child actually has an absentee father."

Another person said, "Given the many things that can attract youngsters and lure them away from the home and the yeshivah, a great deal of skill is necessary in raising children. But are young people capable of doing good parenting? How can they be good parents when they lack the basics of being good husbands and wives?

"Suppose someone comes to a community and wants to take the position of a *shochet* (ritual slaughterer). He will be asked, 'Who says you qualify to be a *shochet*? Where is your *kabbalah* (rabbinical authorization)?' Without proof of qualification, he is not allowed to be a *shochet*. But when a couple comes to the rabbi to schedule their *chuppah* (wedding ceremony) are they asked, 'Where is the evidence that you are qualified to be a parent?' People have children without the slightest idea of what it takes to be a good parent.

"You will say that young people have been getting married and having children for thousands of years without undergoing formal training in parenting. Sure, in the *shtetl* there was no problem. If a child was brought up by the street that was not so bad. The street in the *shtetl* was decent. But today's street is poisonous. Everywhere there are influences that violate all concepts of morality and decency. Today's parents have a great challenge, and many are simply unprepared for it."

Another person said, "I'll tell you why so many young people are drifting away or getting thrown out of yeshivos. The yeshivah simply does not hold their interest.

"I know that many yeshivah instructors are directing their teaching to only one-third of the class. These are the brighter youngsters who can follow the instructor's explanations, and he is interested only in them. The other two-thirds sit there like dummies and have no idea what is going on. Of course they will lose interest in the subject and begin to look elsewhere for something that does interest them. They are bored, impatient and begin to make *shtick* (mischief) that ends up in their getting expelled.

"Expelling a student from a yeshivah is a death sentence. If he is accepted in another yeshivah, his reputation accompanies him. He feels he is expected to live up to his reputation as a troublemaker, and he does.

""I know, because I am a principal in a yeshivah, and I have taken in kids who have been kicked out of other yeshivos. I give these kids special attention. I try to find out why they were not attentive to learning. I meet with the parents and we work out a plan together to help this child.

"You will ask, 'Have I ever expelled a child from my yeshivah?' Yes. On two occasions I had no choice. The child's behavior was endangering other children. But let me tell you a story.

"A major contributor to the Ponivezh yeshivah had an appointment to meet the Rosh Yeshivah, Rav Shach z'tzl. It was the last appointment of the day. He had to wait for an hour because Rav Shach was delayed. Finally, Rav Shach emerged accompanied by a young boy who was holding a *gemara* (volume of Talmud). He apologized to the man and said, 'This young boy was misbehaving in the yeshivah. They asked me what to do, and I felt that he had to be expelled. But now, who would learn with him? So I have him come every day and I learn with him for an hour.'

"The most painful thing in my life is to expel a child. In these two incidents, I made a great effort to meet with the parents, and I arranged for the child to be accepted in another yeshivah. I made a 'going-away' party for the child. I had his teachers present, and each one related some positive thing about the child.

"I then said to the child, 'It hurts me to lose you, but you must understand that because of the way you behaved, I had no choice. You have heard how the teachers related good things about you. You have the ability to be a very good student. In your new school you can have a fresh start. If you run into any problems, you should call me right away,' and I gave him my home number. Both of these boys turned out to be fine *b'nei Torah* (Torah scholars)."

Another person said, "I'm sick and tired of this yeshivah bashing. Our teachers are stretched to the utmost and are underpaid. Many have to hold a second job or do tutoring after school hours to support their families. How much can you expect of a teacher who is exhausted and has to control a large class?

"The problem is not with the school but with the home. Some parents are more concerned about their own reputation than about what is good for the child. If a child doesn't live up to the parents' expectation or he shows the least sign of deviating from the parents' life style, he is immediately made to feel that he is no good.

"Someone asked the Baal Shem Tov what to do about one of his children who was showing signs of rebellion. The Baal Shem Tov said, 'Show him extra special love. He needs it the most.' "

One principal said, "The reason some children lose interest in learning is that they have difficulty in understanding some of the abstract concepts of the Talmud. The child promptly concludes, 'I'm not as smart as the other children. I'm too stupid to understand what others do.' From that point on, his mind is closed. He has given up on himself.

"In my yeshivah we do not begin the day with *gemara*. The first class is a half-hour of *chumash* which all the children can understand. The second class is twenty minutes of discussion of *middos*, accompanied by an interesting story about one of our *gedolim* (great Torah personalities.). By the time we start *gemara*, the child has self-confidence that he can understand Torah.

"At the beginning of the year the teacher tells the class, 'This is too large a class. Within a few days, we are going to break up into two groups.' He is then very attentive to each child's abilities to follow the *gemara*, and by the end of two weeks he knows which are the weaker students. The class is then divided into two classes, but the children are not aware of the basis for the division. The weaker students are spared the embarrassment of being labeled. They are taught *gemara* in a more simplified way. Do you know the result? The students of the stronger class are asking to be allowed to join the weaker class. Of course, this puts an extra burden on the finances of the yeshivah because we must hire more teachers, but I feel it is our responsibility to make every child teachable."

I sat through this meeting without uttering a word. When they asked for my opinion, I said that I had nothing to add. All the problems had been clearly elucidated, and the definition of the problems contained the solutions. All that remained was to implement them.

I have alluded to the importance of self-esteem in developing a healthy personality. Children who deviate from Torah frequently have a low self-esteem which makes them more vulnerable to seduction by anyone or anything that promises to make them feel better. Parents and teachers should do everything possible to strengthen a child's self-esteem. Needless to say, berating or humiliating a child can seriously depress self-esteem. A child can be disciplined effectively without depressing his self-esteem. I addressed this issue at length in *Positive Parenting.*

The *yetzer hara* takes advantage of every opportunity to ruin a child. It will seize upon any of the above factors or other causes not mentioned.

Parents must recognize that our children face unprecedented dangers of drifting away. It can happen and has happened in families where it would be least expected. We must be shaken out of our complacency. It can no longer be "business as usual." All of the points that were mentioned at this meeting must be given serious consideration. Parents and educators must find time to get together and work together for the welfare of every child.

An ounce of prevention is worth many pounds of cure. Parents who are too busy to learn more about parenting and to take the time to attend to their children may find that the time they may have to spend to try to reclaim their child and the distress which results when a child deviates more than justifies restructuring their priorities.

Our children are not only our most prized possession but also our greatest responsibility. Parents should realize that with all their good intentions they may not know all they should about parenting, and should make an effort at increasing their expertise. I believe it would be an enormous benefit to the health of future generations if junior and senior high school students were given a course in parenting. This would enable them to develop parenting skills before they are faced with the actual challenge. Incidentally, it would also be most beneficial if instruction were given about marriage to this same age group. Many young people enter into marriage without the faintest idea of what it means to be a husband or a wife.

It is also extremely important that all teachers receive training in pedagogy. A kollel graduate may be very well versed in Talmud and halachah, but this alone does not guarantee effective teaching techniques.

Raising healthy children in today's world is an unprecedented challenge. Parents and teachers must maximize their skills and resources to give our children the best opportunities for success and happiness.

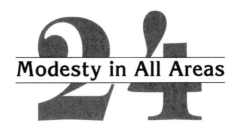

Modesty in All Areas

"What is it that G-d asks of you, but to do justice, love acts of kindness and walk before your G-d with *tzenius*" (*Michah* 6:8). This is generally translated as "walk humbly before your G-d." But this translation is not quite accurate. *Tzenius* is more than humility. It also means "discreet" and "modest." The Talmud also adds the concept of "in privacy" (*Yalkut Balak* 771). *Tzenius* is "all of the above."

Tzenius as modesty has suffered a severe setback in modern times. I recall that when I was 6 years old, even men were not permitted on the beach without a two-piece bathing suit. The exposure that is fashionable today would not have been possible sixty years ago.

Modesty refers to speech as well as to appearance. The obscenity that is heard on the radio, seen on television and read in the printed media was unthinkable and outrageous just several decades ago.

Tzenius requires not only practicing modesty in one's own appearance and speech but also to what one sees and hears. Looking at immodest displays and listening to vulgarity is a violation of *tzenius,* Doubtless, the *yetzer hara* today has made *tzenius* a major challenge.

Tzenius means discreet as well as modest. Dressing in an ostentatious and provocative manner is a violation of *tzenius* even if there is no exposure. Rambam says that a person should dress modestly, neither in rags nor in riches (*Hil. Dei'os* 1:4). This, too, is *tzenius.* A person may certainly enjoy one's wealth, but it is wrong to flaunt it.

There is a concept in Judaism of *ayin hara* (evil eye). It is thought that if one displays one's good fortune before those who are less fortunate, one may be harmed by the latter's *ayin hara* if they begrudge one. Many people think of *ayin hara* as being a superstition. Rabbi Avigdor Miller explained that flaunting one's good fortune before others who are lacking may cause them distress, and it is the lack of consideration of others' feelings for which a person may be held culpable.

A person's behavior should be decent in private as well as in public. The Talmud says that before R' Yochanan ben Zakkai's death his disciples asked for his blessing. R' Yochanan said, "May your fear of G-d equal your fear of other people." He explained that a person may refrain from improper behavior because he would be shamed if others saw him, but may not refrain in private, even though G-d sees him (*Berachos* 28b).

> *The Chafetz Chaim was traveling by horse and wagon. The driver noticed piles of hay in a field and wanted to take some to feed his horse. He asked the Chafetz Chaim to keep a look out and to warn him if anyone was watching. When the driver approached the pile of hay, the Chafetz Chaim shouted, "Someone's watching!" The driver quickly returned to the wagon and drove off.*
>
> *"I didn't notice anyone around," he said.*
>
> *The Chafetz Chaim said, "You told me to warn you if anyone was watching. Well, G-d was watching."*

R' Yochanan ben Zakkai was right.

This concept of *tzenius* has suffered in modern times. People who would be afraid to be seen going into a theater may watch objectionable material on their television sets. In the privacy of their four walls some people may watch obscenity or engage in inappropriate discussions by using the Internet. The latter has caused serious character deterioration and has resulted in marriages being undermined.

How can we defend ourselves against this latest assault by the *yetzer hara?* The prophet answered this when he said, "and walk with *tzenius* before your G-d." We must constantly remind ourselves that we are in the presence of G-d and that He is always watching us. The very first paragraph of the Shulchan Aruch states this principle as a preamble. "A person's behavior in the presence of a king is different than when he is by himself." A true sense of reverence of G-d will militate against improper behavior in privacy. It is well to frequently verbalize the verse, "I always place G-d before me" (*Psalms* 16:8). Today, more than ever, we need to be cognizant of this.

Legalization

The modern *yetzer hara* has resurrected an ancient tool of decadence: legalization. If any improper behavior becomes widespread and appears to be uncontrollable, give up the battle and legalize it.

This is hardly a new technique. It was employed by the biblical cities of Sodom and Gomorrah, whose laws, according to the Midrash, legitimized every abomination. This is why these cities had to be destroyed, and even the Patriarch Abraham's fervent pleas to spare the cities were rejected. If a person is able to discover that what he did was wrong, it is possible that he may amend his ways. Once an improper act is legalized, there is no chance of *teshuvah* (repentance). A person will not repent for what he thinks was permissible and proper.

This insidious tactic of legitimizing wrong is being increasingly applied nowadays. When the first case of physician-assisted suicide was reported, there was a universal expression of outrage. Just several years later, a number of state legislatures have passed laws legalizing physician-assisted suicide. Because all the governmental efforts to stop the drug trade have failed to stop the widespread use of drugs, the proposed solution is: legalize drugs.

In the past, gambling had been considered a vice. Recently, many states have legalized gambling, and casinos have proliferated like mushrooms after a rain. True, casinos are not the cause of compulsive gambling any more than supermarkets are the cause of obesity. Inasmuch as food is necessary to sustain life, there must be food vendors. But gambling is not a necessity of life, and legalizing gambling has made it more easily accessible and respectable. As a result, those people who are vulnerable to compulsive gambling but who might not have sought out a bookie now have no impediment to gambling. Many of these have brought ruin to their families, which might not have happened had gambling remain illegal.

There is great danger in this approach as was made clear by Nazi Germany's legalization of extermination of Jews. If there is no absolute and immutable moral and ethical right and wrong, there is simply no limit to what may be legalized. This is the basic error of those who have tampered with Torah and have tried to legitimize what had been forbidden for centuries. Again, we should not delude ourselves that we are impervious to ideas in our environment.

Rambam says that although one should generally follow "the golden path," i.e. a moderate position between two extremes, it may sometimes be necessary to go toward an extreme to overcompensate for something that has gone to the opposite extreme (*Hil. Dei'os* 2:2).

I have always felt that it is not necessary or desirable to go beyond halachah and look for *chumros* (stringencies that go beyond the basic requirements of halachah). But in the light of the current tendency to legalize what had previously been forbidden, perhaps it would help if we did adopt some restrictions rather than find a *hetter* (halachic sanction) to make things more convenient.

It is interesting that the Talmud complains, "Today's generations are not like previous generations. Earlier generations would go out of their way to bring themselves to do mitzvos, whereas today's generations look for loopholes to evade mitzvos" (*Berachos* 35b).

The Torah requires that one should stand as a sign of respect when a Torah scholar approaches, and concludes with, "and you shall revere your G-d" (*Leviticus* 19:32). The Talmud states that if a person sees a Torah scholar in the distance and closes his eyes so that he will not be obligated to arise when he approaches, he is derelict in reverence of G-d even though he is not in violation of the mitzvah (*Kiddushin* 33a).

I am not equating a halachic *hetter* with legislation that removes a prohibition. The two are very different. A *hetter* does not change halachah. Rather, it is based on demonstrating why a given situation is not prohibited by halachah, which remains intact. However, to outward appearances it may seem that a *hetter* is legalizing what had previously been forbidden. Children, especially, may not be able to distinguish the difference.

For example, there is a very legitimate *hetter* to drink *chalav akum* (milk lacking kosher supervision). Under other circumstances, there would be nothing wrong with relying on this *hetter*. But, given the current secular propensity to legalize everything, perhaps it might be wise not to avail ourselves of this *hetter*. The same thinking would apply to other things for which there may be a legitimate *hetter*. This is one way in which we can demonstrate to our children that we do not seek to change traditional Torah practices.

As pointed out earlier, there may be a need today for countermaneuvers that were not necessary in past years.

Alcohol and Substance Abuse

The aphorism, "*Shikker* (a drunkard) is a *goy* (non-Jew),"
had actual basis in fact. Traditionally, drunkenness
was repudiated by Jews. There may have been a village
drunkard, a pathetic soul who was recognized to be a sick
person. True, Jews celebrated with a *"L'chaim,"* but rarely did
drinking get out of hand.

The traditional aphorism is no longer true. The incidence
of alcoholism among Jews has increased.

It is difficult to abtain accurate statistics about a condition
that is generally kept under wraps, but have no doubt about
it. As an expert in the field, I can testify that alcoholism
among Jews is not a rarity.

Perhaps the best indication of this increase is the fact that
in the past, country clubs refused to accept booking for a bar-
mitzvah party or a "Jewish" wedding. Country clubs make
their profit on the drinks rather than on the food, and Jewish
affairs were simply not profitable. Today, country clubs
clamor for Jewish business.

Various theories have been proposed for the increased
consumption of alcohol among Jews, and all may be

contributing factors. In all probability, the Rambam has been proven right again: we are heavily influenced by our environment, and we live in a society where excessive drinking prevails.

The most consistent symptom of alcoholism is *denial.* For a variety of psychological reasons, an alcoholic is unable to admit to himself, let alone to others, that his drinking is excessive and destructive. Furthermore, the family of the alcoholic, although they may be suffering due to the person's drinking, may also be in denial.

Among Jews, the denial of alcoholism is even greater than among non-Jews. To be an alcoholic is a *shondeh* (a horrible disgrace). As loathsome as thievery is, there was never an aphorism, " A *goniff* (thief) is a *goy.*" To be a *shikker* was considered worse than to be a sinner, and was considered to be totally outside the realm of Judaism. It is unthinkable for a Jew to consider himself to be a *shikker.* As a result of the refusal or inability to recognize the problem, everyone dances around it and virtually no one does anything about it.

About twenty-five years ago, a small group made an effort to bring about greater awareness of this problem and facilitate Jews to get help. Their efforts have been rewarded, but it is still an uphill battle. For example, JACS (Jewish **A**lcoholics, **C**hemically-dependent and **S**ignificant others) is trying to get synagogues to open their doors to meetings of Alcoholics Anonymous, but the resistance is formidable. Many rabbis are closed minded to the social illnesses among Jews. If there are alcoholics, cocaine addicts or wife batterers among Jews, it can only be in other communities, but not among their membership.

The *yetzer hara* has capitalized on the increase in drinking among Jews and on the across-the-board denial of the problem. Families are being ruined, young people often progress from alcohol to drugs and incalculable misery results. The *yetzer hara* gloats in its triumph.

This problem calls for radical steps in order to curb this increasing cancer. First, rabbis and community leaders must take off their blinders and face reality. Rabbis should learn more about alcoholism, how to recognize it and where to send people for help. They should speak about the problem from the pulpit. The officers of the synagogue should open the doors for meetings of Alcoholics Anonymous.

Second, the excessive drinking that frequently occurs in *kiddush clubs* must be stopped. I have seen people come from the social hall at the shul following the conclusion of the prayers visibly intoxicated. There are horror stories about what happens when the husband-father comes home and drinks even more. It is destructive for children to see their father's face fall into the *cholent*, and the abusive behavior that occurs is even worse.

A *L'chaim* is fine. Excessive drinking is not.

The Midrash cites the verse in the Torah that when Noah emerged from the ark, he planted a vineyard. The Midrash relates that Satan came along to help him. He fertilized the vines with the blood of a lamb, then with the blood of a lion, then with the blood of a monkey and finally with the blood of a pig. Therefore, the Midrash states, if a person takes one drink, he becomes calm and meek as a lamb. After the second drink he becomes bold and aggressive as a lion. With the third drink he acts as foolishly as a monkey, and with the fourth drink he becomes as loathsome as a pig (*Tanchuma, Noah*). The Midrash is right on target.

Rabbis and shul officers who allow excessive drinking to go on in shul are grossly derelict in their duties and must be held culpable for the harm that this excessive drinking causes.

The attitude, *"Shikker* is a *goy,"* must be reinstated and made into a reality by eliminating drunkenness from among Jews, *There is no occasion on which excessive drinking should be sanctioned,*

I meet with the objection, "But isn't it a requirement to get drunk on Purim?" My answer is a resounding and unequivocal "**NO!**" Our authority is Rema, who states that by drinking just a bit more than one is accustomed to, and then taking a nap, one will thereby fulfill the requirement of not distinguishing between "Cursed is Haman and blessed is Mordechai" (*Orach Chaim* 695:2). The Chafetz Chaim in *Mishnah Berurah* (§5) comments, "This is the proper thing to do." Anyone who wishes to surpass the piety of the Chafetz Chaim and drink more than the *Mishnah Berurah* designates must prove that he is equally superior to the Chafetz Chaim in all other aspects of his behavior.

I call upon the rabbis and heads of yeshivos to curtail excessive drinking at weddings, Simchas Torah and Purim. It is not that everyone who gets drunk on Purim is alcoholic. Rather, because of the disastrous consequences of excessive drinking and its increasing prevalence, especially among young people, it is necessary to emphatically demonstrate that excessive drinking is loathsome, non-Jewish and will simply not be condoned.

The proliferation of drugs among Jewish youth is alarming. Many young people have begun the destructive use of drugs with marijuana. Some have progressed to more harmful and addictive drugs, often with manifest, rapid deterioration. These may lead to brain damage and even death. *Although marijuana does not produce such dramatic destruction, it is not a safe drug.* Especially in young people, marijuana can cause a "amotivational syndrome," in which they lose interest and ambition. They may waste the most important years of their lives in aimless drifting, and by the time they come to their senses, the golden period of education and preparation for life has passed.

Understandably, the *yetzer hara* has exploited the drug scene to destroy young people. This is a modern Amalek which the earlier works of *mussar* did not address.

What should be done to combat this vicious Amalek? First, there must be an increased awareness that *there is no immunity.* Young people from the finest Torah-observant homes have fallen into the trap of drug addiction. Parents should be on the alert and know what are the early signs of drug use and what to do when these are suspected. They should also familiarize themselves with the terminology of drugs and what their effects are. Enlightened parents may able to detect drug use in its early stages. The resource that I recommend most highly is: *Children in Crisis-Detection and Intervention.* (*Nefesh,* ed. Russell and Blumenthal).

Some parents may have a false sense of security. "*Baruch Hashem,* my sons are in yeshivah and my daughters are in Beis Yaakov. I don't have to worry about drugs." Remember, you protected your children against diseases such as polio and whooping cough by having the doctor give them immunizing injections. In spite of the fine education your children are receiving, *the risk of their using drugs is greater than getting polio or whooping cough.* Unfortunately, we do not have anything to immunize them, and we must do second best by being alert and knowledgeable.

Second, we should realize that when children are frustrated in school, the risk of their turning to drugs is increased. Some of the causes for such frustration were noted earlier (in Chapter 23, "The Severest Wound). The crucial importance of elevating a child's self-esteem was also noted.

Third, we should know that scare techniques do not deter young people from drug use. If they want the "high" of drugs, they will not be discouraged by the long-term destructive consequences.

Just a bit of thinking will make us realize that this is *precisely the mentality of the cigarette smoker.* It is well known that cigarettes can cause lung cancer, emphysema and increased risk of heart attacks. The person who smokes cigarettes is making the statement that he is willing to accept the risk of these long-term effects in order to get the pleasure of smoking. This is a powerful modeling for drug use.

Furthermore, it is extremely rare to find a drug-using youngster who had not been using cigarettes first. *Non-smoking youngsters rarely become drug users.* If people whom a youngster admires and respects smoke, they are sanctioning — if not encouraging — the use of cigarettes and are contributing to the likelihood of that youngster smoking and lowering his resistance to drug use. Parents, grand-parents and teachers should be aware of the awesome effects their smoking may have on their children, grandchildren and students.

Some people may say, "But it is so hard to stop smoking. I tried and could not do it." These are exactly what young people say about marijuana and other drugs. We must show them that it is possible to do something that is difficult and uncomfortable.

If parents discover that their child is using drugs, they should promptly turn to a competent drug counselor for help on how to relate to the child. Utilizing their own ideas as to how to react to the child can be disastrous. Their well-intentioned response may aggravate the problem. Many psychologists, psychiatrists and rabbis have not had training in drug abuse problems and their advice may be counter-productive. Only a counselor with experience in drug abuse cases should be consulted.

Alcoholism and drug use are almost invariably the result of what we have referred to earlier as a "spirituality deficiency syndrome," the primary symptom of which is a pervasive and persistent feeling of discontent. This is so uncomfortable that people will do virtually anything for relief. Alcohol and drugs, by numbing the brain, anesthetize a person so that one does not feel the discontent.

The ultimate answer to the substance abuse problem is eliminating the discontent, which can only be done by providing the missing spirituality. Observance of Torah and mitzvos should accomplish this, but alas! The prophet Isaiah bewailed the loss of spirituality by those who observe Torah and mitzvos out of habit, without a true passion for their bringing one into a more intimate relationship with G-d. From time to time there have been infusions of spirit and passion into Torah observance. The sages of the Talmud instituted *berachos* (blessings) as prefatory to the study of Torah and performance of mitzvos, but before long, we began verbalizing these *berachos* with very little feeling. In the more recent past, the Baal Shem Tov through *chassidus* and R' Yisroel of Salant through *mussar* injected new fire into Torah and mitzvos. But again the *yetzer hara* triumphed, and these two inspiring philosophies have lost much of their passion.

There is only one thing left. The last Mishnah in *Sotah*, which describes the tragic conditions that will prevail prior to the ultimate redemption, closes with, "And we can depend only on our Father in heaven." He is a source of infinite strength and inspiration. We must fervently ask Him to instill within us the passion to serve Him and to bring us closer to Him.

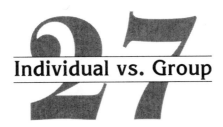

Individual vs. Group

One of the problems of the super-industrialized world is that much individuality has been lost. In the past, a craftsman could take pride in the product of his labors. Today, much of manufacturing is mass production. It is more economical for each person to produce a large number of the same part. The parts are then assembled to make the finished product, but no one person can claim credit for the whole product.

Mass production did not stop with manufacturing. Although perhaps not mass produced, news and information is delivered by the mass media, so that millions of people hear and often believe what a few people want them to believe. Inasmuch as a person can form an opinion only with the information one has, relatively few people develop their own opinions about anything.

Education has also been affected by mass production. Many educational institutions have enrollments of thousands of students, all of whom are to a greater or lesser degree influenced by the school policy and attitudes.

This is true of yeshivos as well. The Chazon Ish said that yeshivos have saved the *klal* (multitude) but have sacrificed the *prat* (individual). There are various styles and orientations to Torah study, and many yeshivah students are molded by the approach of the head of the yeshivah. A student may not be able to discover and pursue his unique way of thinking, and individuality is stifled.

This is what Solomon meant: "Educate a young person according to *his* way" (*Proverbs* 22:6). Encourage and cultivate his uniqueness. Do not try to mold him into your way.

I was privileged to know many first-generation immigrants. They had not been subjected to the mass media or mass education, and no two of them were alike. They were delightful and charming characters because each one was unique. Today, people tend to be like tin soldiers, pressed from a single mold. (Of course, we are not discussing matters of halachah, where conformity is mandatory, or those customs which have halachic status.) But beyond such matters, legitimate individuality should not be stifled.

> *It is related that as a young man, the rebbe R' Shalom Shachna, a grandson-in-law of the rebbe of Chernobel (and the father of R' Yisroel of Rizhin), was not following the practices of Chernobler chassidus. The chassidim complained to the rebbe, who asked him why he was behaving this way.*
>
> *R' Shalom Shachna replied, "The egg of a duck got mixed up with the eggs that a chicken was hatching. When the duck came out of the eggshell, it was different than the chicks. One time the mother hen was walking along the edge of a lake, and the duckling jumped into the water. The mother hen shouted, 'Come back! You will drown!' The duckling responded, 'Don't worry, Mother. I know how to swim.'"* The rebbe then told his *chassidim to leave the young man to his own ways.*

We should get to know our children and students well enough to know whether they are capable of a healthy, halachically acceptable non-conformity. If they are, we should not discourage their individuality.

At Sinai, G-d said to the Israelites, "*Anochi Hashem Elokecha,* I am your G-d," using the Hebrew singular for "your" although addressing a multitude. The commentaries give two explanations for this. (1) The entire congregation of Israel was united and could be addressed as if they were a single unit; and (2) G-d was addressing each person individually.

Both interpretations are true. We should be thoroughly united and relate to G-d and to each other as a *klal*, but we should retain our individuality as a *prat*.

If a person loses his individuality, he allows other people to think for him and even to determine who he is. He has no personality of his own and changes like a chameleon to accommodate and please everyone. Failure to be oneself may give rise to psychological problems.

This is especially important today, when we live in an environment that has weakened its moral and ethical standards. If a person does something that he knows is wrong, he should not be lulled into tranquility by the fact that the culture thinks it is permissible. This is what the Talmud meant, "Even if the entire world tells you are right, you should think of yourself as wrong" (*Niddah* 30b). Keep an open mind, listen to other opinions, accept the rulings of competent Torah authorities, but do not surrender your uniqueness.

Songs of the Heart

"And it was when the musician played, the spirit of G-d rested upon him" (*II Kings* 3:15).

Music has always been an important component of Divine service. The Levites had to undergo years of training before they could participate in the choir and orchestra in the Temple. King David composed the psalms with the accompaniment of the harp. Traditional melodies of the prayers have been sung in synagogues for centuries. No one can remain unmoved by the strains of Kol Nidrei.

More recently, chassidic masters composed *nigunim* (melodies) to parts of the liturgy. The beautiful compositions of the rebbes of Modzhitz, Melitz, Bobov, Skulen and others enhance the psalms and prayers. There are melodies of *deveikus* (profound meditation). Their joyous melodies express the *simchah* (joy) on the festivals and at weddings.

Secular music, too, has great beauty. The profound masterpieces of Beethoven, the relaxing waltz melodies of Strauss and the majestic marches of Sousa are enchanting.

However, in recent years secular music has undergone a radical change. A new variety of music has appeared which is associated with drugs, violence and immorality. The band leaders that young people worship may be drug addicted, and some of the stars are notorious for their moral corruption. Some music festivals have turned into abominable orgies. This new music has had very negative influences on young people.

Judaism should have repelled this new music and made it as repulsive as pork. But lo and behold! Instead of repudiating it, we now have Jewish "rock," played at deafening decibels. Music which does anything but uplift the spirit has been set to the sacred verses of the psalm. The *yetzer hara*, always on the lookout for ways in which to corrupt our youth, has scored a victory. We can well understand the Talmudic statement that "the Torah girds itself in sackcloth and complains to G-d, 'Your children have made me into an instrument played by scoffers' " (*Sanhedrin* 101a).

Inappropriate rock music does not become kosher when the verses of Psalms are incorporated. To the contrary, these sacred verses are defiled by music which arouses the most objectionable human traits.

Our young people must resist the lure and challenges of the secular world, with its deadly pursuit of drug-induced "highs." Music inspired by and conducive to these destructive behaviors has no place in Judaism.

Infants do not come into the world with a taste for a particular type of music. This is learned, and we must take care to what we expose our children. The Talmud states that the mother of R' Yehoshua ben Chananya put his crib near the *beis midrash* (hall of study) so that the first sounds coming to the infant's ears should be the words and melodies of Torah and *tefillah* (prayer). Parents can help their children develop a fondness for true Jewish music.

When I was a child, there were no tapes of chassidic music, but I grew up with the chants of *chazzanim* (cantors), who interpreted the prayers with heartfelt strains. How unfortunate that so few of our young people today appreciate *chazzanus.*

Infants are comforted by music. Parents should take care that true, inspirational Jewish music is what their young children are hearing. Jewish concerts are fine, but should not feature the kind of music which will cause the Torah to don sackcloth and complain to G-d that it is being abused by His children.

Unwise Neglect

S elf-survival is one of the strongest human instincts, surpassed only by the parental love for a child. It is, therefore, most surprising that people neglect themselves and their children whom they dearly love. Such neglect runs counter to human instincts and can be only the doings of the *yetzer hara*, which achieves its destructive goal by deluding people.

How else can one explain the use of cigarettes by people who love life and dread the thought of suffering, becoming disabled or dying? People are aware of the very toxic aware of cigarettes. It is only the work of the *yetzer hara*, which caused the first sin and unleashed the Angel of Death when it told Eve not to heed the word of G-d that the fruit of the Tree of Knowledge would kill them. "The serpent (*yetzer hara*) said to the woman, 'You will not surely die' " (*Genesis* 3:4). The *yetzer hara* succeeded in deluding Eve, and it has continued its success in deluding people. "Satan, the *yetzer hara*, and the Angel of Death are one and the same" (*Bava Basra* 16a). It tempts, entices, deludes and kills.

I have watched, usually helplessly, how parents allow children with serious conditions to go untreated. First, the *yetzer hara* blinds them to what is happening before their eyes. They do not see what should be obvious. Second, if they do discover that something is wrong, the *yetzer hara* convinces them that they should not do anything about it. "It will get better by itself." "If your child goes for treatment, it will hurt his/her chances for a *shidduch* (marriage)." "When he/she gets married, everything will straighten out." These and similar excuses allow dangerous conditions to progress untreated.

We can consider this a modern-day problem. We do not know the reason why, but there are clearly more cases of Obsessive-Compulsive Disorder (OCD), various types of depression and anorexia/bulimia than ever before. I have seen this increase over forty years of psychiatric practice.

It may shock you to know that anywhere between 15-25 percent of adolescent young women suffer from some degree of anorexia/bulimia. Many young women fear that a little extra weight will make them unattractive, and their fear is not completely groundless. *Shadchanim* (marriage brokers) have told me that when they suggest a young woman for a young man, the very first thing the latter's mother asks is, "What size dress does she wear?" The first question is not about the young woman's *middos*. It is almost certain that a response of size 10 or above will result in "I'm not interested." With this attitude prevailing, it is little wonder that many young women panic if they gain a few pounds.

The first thing these young women do is try to control their diet. This gives the *yetzer hara* the opportunity to apply the tactic espoused by King Solomon, "Forbidden waters are sweet"(*Proverbs* 9:17). They succumb to the craving for food, and then try to undo the harm by fasting, strenuous exercise, purging with laxatives or forced vomiting. They are generally able to maintain their desired weight, but at an exorbitant cost. In addition to their weight-reduction maneuvers, their minds are preoccupied all day with thoughts about food. Some young women, under this constant tension, may lapse into a clinical depression.

These young women generally manage to keep their problem secret from unsuspecting parents. If the parents do discover the problem, they are likely to try to reason with the young woman but will not consider professional help because it may affect the young woman's *shidduch* chances. The *yetzer hara* blinds them to the fact that the untreated condition may have a much greater negative effect on *shidduchim*.

Eating disorders of any kind should not be neglected. Crash diets and gimmicks do not work for the long term. I discussed these problems at some length in *The Thin You Within You.* Parents should be alert to detect eating disorders and seek competent help.

Another condition which is too often neglected is post-partum depression. I was invited to lecture to a large Jewish community because of some tragic consequences of post-Partum Depressions that had occurred. Young mothers may be reluctant to admit that they are depressed and may try to struggle through this condition. Parents may try to help, not realizing that even their helpful support may not be enough, because the condition is a biochemical disorder which requires treatment.

In many Jewish families, the possibility that one may require antidepressant medication precipitates a panic reaction with fierce resistance. Depriving a person suffering from clinical or postpartum depression of appropriate medical treatment is like depriving a pneumonia patient of antibiotics. This is not only most foolish, but frankly criminal. Very serious consequences may result. Further elaboration on this theme may be found in *Getting Up When You're Down.*

In the latter book, I also discussed OCD. This is a condition characterized by persistent doubting and an inability to accept reassurance, intrusive thoughts and/or repeated rituals. There is reason to believe that this condition has a biochemical basis. However, the symptoms of the condition are generally related to personal ideas. In Torah-observant people, the symptoms of OCD are generally of a religious nature. Consequently, it may be thought that the person is being meticulously religious rather than having a psychological disorder. The *yetzer hara* exploits this confusion to prevent the person from receiving appropriate treatment.

In rather extreme cases it is obvious that the problem is OCD. However, there may be a gray area in which it may be difficult to determine whether it is piety or OCD. For example, a person may be very meticulous about *netilas yodayim* (ritual washing of the hands). This may fall into the range of religious scrupulosity. However, if the repeated hand-washing results in abrasions of the skin and bleeding, it is far beyond what Torah requires.

Separation of meat and dairy is the practice in observant homes. However, if a woman repeatedly throws out dishes because she thinks that the towel with which they were dried had accidentally been put in the meat drawer rather than the dairy drawer, this is not in any way Torah observance. Characteristically, the woman has the husband put the *shaaleh* (religious question) before a *posek* (halachic authority). When the husband reports that the *posek* said it is kosher, the woman says that he did not state the question accurately. She then calls the *posek*, and upon receiving a "kosher" ruling, says that the *posek* did not understand her well, and she proceeds to throw out the dishes. This is a psychological problem rather than religious scrupulosity.

Milder cases of OCD are too often overlooked. This is an error, because the symptoms are often progressive.

Some people are tormented by doubts or indecent

thoughts. The more they try to banish these from their minds, the more they recur with increased force. The person may not be able to concentrate on work or study. If the condition is not recognized, one may be advised to pray more fervently, say more *tehillim* (psalms) and study *mussar* writings. In cases of OCD, such advice may aggravate the condition. In such instances, the *yetzer hara* may masquerade as a *tzaddik*, chastising a person for not being sufficiently *frum* (pious).

It is important that parents resist the deluding tactics of the *yetzer hara*. Parents should be alert to their children's behavior, and if something appears to be "just not right," *they* should consult a competent mental health specialist. It is not necessary to promptly take a child to a therapist. The parents should seek advice from a therapist first. They may be told, "Leave it alone. It's just a passing fad." They may be advised that they should have some guidance how to manage the child's behavior. If it is necessary that the child be seen, the therapist will recommend this.

We love our children. When they are infants, we take them to the doctor for immunization because we wish to protect their health. The same interest should apply to protecting them from emotional disorders.

Having mentioned parents' concern about *shidduchim*, I must add that the *yetzer hara* has found an additional way to create misery. It counsels parents to withhold information which may deter a *shidduch*. Withholding such information is as unconscionable as it is sinful. The Chafetz Chaim considers this a violation of "Do not put a stumbling block before the blind" (*Leviticus* 19:14). Furthermore, the Chafetz Chaim says that if a person knows that there is a problem with either partner to the *shidduch*, and that knowledge of this problem would make the other partner reconsider, one is obligated, under certain circumstances, to reveal information even without being asked. Not revealing such information is a violation of "Do not stand idly by while your fellow's blood is being shed" (*Leviticus* 19:16).

What does the *yetzer hara* gain from advising parents to withhold important information? Let me demonstrate with a case.

A young woman suffered several episodes of mania and depression before age 20. Fearing that disclosing this would ruin a *shidduch,* her family withheld the information.

Two weeks before her wedding, the young woman suffered a depressive episode. It was all the family could do to virtually drag her to the wedding. The husband, a rather naive *yeshivah bachur*, attributed her behavior to the adjustment to marriage. Several months later, the husband's parents visited and were alarmed by what they saw. They had the young woman consult a psychiatrist, and the history of the episodes in her adolescence emerged. The husband and his parents were outraged that this information had been withheld. They felt that the marriage was fraudulent. A *beis din* agreed with them and ordered a *get*. By this time the woman was expecting a child.

What had been accomplished by withholding the information to avoid deterring a *shidduch*? The young woman was a divorcee, the young man had undergone an emotional trauma, and perhaps worst of all, a child was brought into the world under the most unfavorable circumstances. Three people and their families had been crushed with one blow. This was a major triumph for the *yetzer hara*.

The young woman's parents certainly had her best interests at heart. There are only two internal sources that provide counseling: the *yetzer tov* and the *yetzer hara*. It is inconceivable that the *yetzer tov* would counsel to do something unethical and against the halachic rulings of the Chafetz Chaim. Their decision to withhold information could only have emanated from the *yetzer hara*, whose powers of duping are formidable.

My heart breaks for parents when they call me with this problem. "Our son/daughter had this particular problem, which is either being treated or is in remission but there is a possibility of recurrences. If we reveal it, the chances for a good *shidduch* are nil. What should we do?"

These parents realize that if the other side had withheld important information from them, they would have been furious. Yet, their desire to prevent their child from being unhappy affects their judgment. The *yetzer hara* seizes this opportunity to mislead them.

There are many aspects of reality that are unpleasant. One person said, "I have learned to live in the world the way it is rather than the way I'd like it to be."

One young woman consulted me because she had a condition which she said she would never conceal. "I realize that I have this defect. I know I will be unable to get the best *shidduch*. I will have to marry someone with a defect. What I would like to know is what are the things I should overlook."

I marveled at this young woman's courage and integrity, and I share this with parents who ask my opinion.

We must accept reality for what it is and resist the counsel of the *yetzer hara*. It always tells us to take the short-term gain and not consider the long-term loss. We must be wise to its tactics.

The Enemy's Ruse

R'Eliyahu Dessler says that in order to triumph in the battle with the *yetzer hara* we must understand the strategies it employs (*Michtav M'Eliyahu* vol.3 p.38). I will share with you something I have garnered in my work with alcoholics.

Alcoholics Anonymous describes alcohol as "an enemy; cunning, baffling and powerful." This is a very apt description of the *yetzer hara*. The way the *yetzer hara* undermines one's resolve is very similar to the way an alcoholic relapses.

In treatment, the alcoholic is told that he must avoid "people, places and things" that were associated with his drinking. He must remain in close contact with a sober support group and engage a person with long sobriety to be his "sponsor" or adviser.

Here is the way relapse often occurs. After leaving treatment, the alcoholic may have no desire for drink. "You could put a bottle in front of me and I wouldn't even touch it." This is the stratagem of the "enemy alcohol;" avoid causing a craving to lull the person into a false sense of security.

After a period free of craving, the alcoholic may wish to join his former drinking buddies, not to drink with them, but just for the camaraderie. These friends welcome him, and while they drink beer, he orders a diet Pepsi. He then thinks, "There is nothing wrong with being with my old friends. It did not cause me to drink." Again, the "enemy alcohol" has given him a false sense of security.

Eventually the alcoholic thinks, "If I can sit with my drinking friends and not drink, that means that I have overcome my problem. It is now safe for me to have just one beer." He does so, and when he does not progress to intoxication, he is convinced that he is over his problem. He no longer needs to attend regular meetings of his support group and follow the guidance of his sponsor.

This is what the "enemy alcohol" has planned from the onset. Soon the person deteriorates into full-blown alcoholic drinking again.

This is the way the *yetzer hara* operates. It does not begin by launching a frontal attack. It lulls the person into a false sense of security. He allows himself to fraternize with non-Jews. "They will not cause me to eat nonkosher." This association leads to familiarity and to improper relationships. "I can watch the sitcoms safely. They will not corrupt me," but the obscenity and immorality penetrate into one's thoughts. "Watching violence will not cause me to act violently," but one loses control of anger and acts out in rage.

We have support groups: *minyan* (communal prayer), *daf yomi* (daily Talmud study). The *yetzer hara* leads one to think, "I have to get to work early or to stay late. Missing *minyan* or *daf yomi* will not hurt me."

The Talmud says, "Make someone into your teacher." The *yetzer hara* says, "You don't need a mentor. You are perfectly capable of making sound judgments."

Our greatest *tzaddikim* feared overconfidence. They constantly engaged in soul-searching, always looking for where they might have fallen short in their service of G-d. The great Gaon of Vilna, with his incomparable knowledge of Torah and peerless piety, engaged someone to give him reprimand.

We cannot relinquish our guard against the *yetzer hara*. It is unrelenting. As Rabbeinu Bachya Ibn Pekuda states:

> Son of man! You should be aware that the greatest enemy you have in the world is your *yetzer*, which is incorporated into the capacities of your soul, is combined with your spirit and which is joined into all your physical and spiritual senses. It dominates in the innermost recesses of your mind. It advises you in all your actions, both the revealed and the hidden, that they should follow your will. It lies in ambush to seduce your steps. You sleep, but it is awake. You may ignore it, but it never ignores you (*Duties of the Heart, Yichud HaMaaseh*, Chapter 5).

That the *yetzer hara* participates in everything we do is demonstrated by this charming anecdote.

> When R' Levi Yitzchok of Berditchev married, his father-in-law was proud that he had so great a Torah scholar for a son-in-law. On Simchas Torah, R' Levi Yitzchok was honored with the reciting of the prayer Atah Hareisa. To everyone's surprise, R' Levi Yitzchok donned the talis (prayer shawl) and removed it several times. Finally, he put the talis down and exclaimed, "If you are so great, then you say Atah Hareisa!" and walked away. The father-in-law was embarrassed by this odd behavior and demanded an explanation.
>
> R' Levi Yitzchok said, "When I put on the talis to say Atah Hareisa, I discovered that the yetzer hara was there. 'What are you doing here?' I asked. The yetzer hara said, 'Why, I want to say Atah Hareisa together with you.' I said, 'But I was given this honor because I am a Torah scholar.' The yetzer hara said, 'When you

studied Torah I was right there with you. I know as much as you do.' I said, 'But I am a chassid, a disciple of the great Maggid of Mezritch.' The yetzer hara responded, 'I was with you at the Maggid, and I am a chassid, too.' That is why I put down the talis and said to the yetzer hara, 'All right! If you are a Torah scholar and a chassid, then you say Atah Hareisa.' "

I believe that R' Levi Yitzchok felt that the honor he was given to lead the congregation in *Atah Hareisa* gave the *yetzer hara* an opening to make him feel vain as a Torah scholar. His teaching was that we must always be on the alert for the *yetzer hara's* wile. As Rabbeinu Bachya said, "It joins in all your physical and spiritual senses."

R' Dessler was right. We must be wise to the insidious maneuvers of the *yetzer hara*. It is a formidable enemy, cunning, baffling and powerful.

Getting Out of the Way

In many places in our prayers, we find statements such as "Give us a virtuous desire to serve You with honesty, with awe and with love," or "May it be Your will that You accustom us to study Your Torah and attach us to Your commandments ... Let not the evil inclination (*yetzer hara*) dominate us ... Attach us to the good inclination (*yetzer tov*) and to good deeds and compel our evil inclination to be subservient to You." Prayers such as these raise the question: How can we ask of G-d to make us do good and avoid evil? This is an issue of *bechirah* (free choice) in which G-d does not intervene. "Everything is in the hands of G-d except for the fear of G-d" (*Berachos* 33b).

Commentaries have tried to deal with this in various ways. I achieved a bit of insight from a remark made by one of my clients. This is a man whose life had been devastated by alcohol and drug abuse, and he then made a remarkable recovery, surprising himself as well as all others who had despaired of him. One day he said, "There is no way I could have recovered by my own efforts. I know that G-d gave me my recovery. He tried to do this many times before. Finally, *I got out of His way.*"

I reflected on this man's words. There is a constant emanation of goodness from G-d. If we do not receive it, it is because we have set up barriers between G-d and ourselves, and we are thwarting His efforts. Even the refinement of our *middos* cannot be of our own doing. G-d will do it for us *if we let Him.* This may well be the intent of the Talmud: "A person's *yetzer* (evil inclination) gains over him every day, and if not that G-d was helping him, one could not withstand it" (*Kiddushin* 30b).

We may be aware that G-d has been persistent in trying to help us, but we have been resisting his aid. Lest we despair of His help, thinking, "How can I expect Him to help me now when I have rejected and resisted His help so many times?" we say the above prayers to remind us that G-d never tires of helping us. He will always continue to help us, but we *must get out of His way* and let His help reach us.

What is the barrier that prevents G-d's help from reaching us? It is our self-centeredness, which is manifested by making gratification of our desires the primary goal of our lives. We can remove this barrier by self-effacement. This does not mean that we must think of ourselves as insignificant and unworthy. To the contrary, we must think of ourselves as worthy of G-d's benevolence, but we must divest ourselves of our ego drives.

Part of the formula for the alcoholic's recovery is the realization that giving in to his will resulted in his ruination, and that he cannot rely on his own will to act constructively. This is exactly what the Talmud tells us is essential for an ethical life: "Nullify your will before His will" (*Ethics of the Fathers* 2:4).

There is great wisdom in substituting G-d's will for our own. Two children received Chanukah *gelt* (money). One ran off to the candy and toy stores and spent all his money there. The excess of candy resulted in a stomach ache, and after several days some of the toys were broken and the rest were relegated to the toy heap with the others in which he had lost interest.

The other child gave the money to his father to put away for him. The father invested the money for him, which proceeded to increase in value.

The first child followed his own will. The second child was wiser and realized that his father's will for him was far better than his own. It behooves us to be wise and to recognize that by following our own will we may experience very transient pleasure, whereas if we substitute G-d's will for our own, we will be far better off.

Let me share with you a story that I heard from my father many times that taught me something about how the ego drives affect spirituality.

> R' Shneur Zalman, author of the basic Chassidic text, Tanya, was puzzled by a particular portion of the Talmud. He knocked on the door of his master, R' Dov of Mezeritch.
>
> "Who is there?" R' Dov asked.
>
> "It is I," R' Zalman answered.
>
> Recognizing the voice, the master said, "Come in, Zalman."
>
> R' Dov listened to the problem and explained the Talmudic passage to his disciple. Then, totally un-expectedly he said, "Have a safe trip, Zalman."
>
> R' Zalman was totally bewildered. A safe trip? He had no intention of going anywhere. However, if the master bid him farewell, then he must go. Whereto? He did not have the faintest notion.
>
> R' Zalman packed his few belongings and set out on the road. As he was passing along the countryside, he heard someone calling, "Hey, you! Wait there!" A man

approached him and said, "We are having a bris (circumcision ceremony). We need a minyan (a quorum of ten required for certain rituals). We are only nine. Please join us." R' Zalman gladly obliged.

After the ritual, R' Zalman was invited to partake of the festive meal. Following the meal, the hostess announced that she had counted the silverware and there was a silver spoon missing. All eyes turned to the stranger as the obvious suspect. "Look here," the host said. "we are grateful that you joined us to make up the minyan, but you have no right to steal anything. Please return the silver spoon. We will be glad to give you alms if you are needy."

"But I did not take any silver spoon," R' Zalman protested.

"Of course you did," the host said. "All the other people here are my close friends and are scrupulously honest. It was obviously you who took the spoon."

"No, it was not I," R' Zalman said.

"Yes, it was you," the host said. "Now admit it and return the spoon."

"But it was not I," R' Zalman said.

Seeing that he was not getting anywhere with words, the host delivered a sharp slap to R' Zalman's face. "You lie!" He said. "It was you."

"It was not I," R' Zalman said.

Seeing the plight of the hosts, the other guests assisted him in beating R' Zalman, who kept protesting, "It was not I."

One of the hired kitchen help, seeing how cruelly R' Zalman was being beaten, could not tolerate it and said, "Leave him alone! I took the spoon," returning it to the host.

The host and guests apologized profusely to R' Zalman and asked his forgiveness.

Upon leaving the house, R' Zalman reflected, "I had had no intention of going anywhere. The master's sending me away could only be because I deserved a punishment. Now that I have received what was due me, I may return to the master."

Upon his return, R' Dov greeted his disciple. "How many times did you say, 'It is not I,' Zalman?"

"Many, many times," R' Zalman said.

R' Dov asked, "When you knocked on the door and I asked who it was, you said 'It is I.' Do you remember that, Zalman?"

"Yes," R' Zalman replied.

"Zalman, a person of your spirituality should know that only G-d has the right to say, 'It is I.' G-d began speaking to the Israelites at Sinai by saying, 'It is I, the Lord your G-d, Who delivered you from the bondage of Egypt.' A human being who says, 'It is I', is displaying a feeling of vanity. That is not becoming for someone like you. For you to say. 'It is I', was a transgression. You had to atone for that transgression by repeatedly saying, 'It is not I.'"

I heard this story first at age 6, and many times thereafter. As I began studying psychology and learning something about the human ego, this story took on new significance. Obviously, there are times when we must use the pronoun "I." But properly understood, we should think of it as "i" rather than the capital "I" and certainly not as a bold "I."

Perhaps we cannot aspire to the spirituality of R' Zalman and so totally efface ourselves that we should not think of ourselves as "I." However, there is much we can do to divest ourselves of our ego drives. We can begin by setting aside our own preferences both in adherence to Torah restrictions and in being devoted to doing things for others. We can then "get out of His way" and allow G-d to bring us to the state of perfection which only He can.

A Healthy Personality

Among the destructive ego drives is that of desiring acclaim and recognition. We have noted that the *mussar* writings consider vanity the worst of all character traits. Rambam considers spiritual defects as "*diseases* of the spirit" (*Shemoneh Perakim* 3-4). Let us see why.

Think for a moment about your ears, elbows, or throat. Now, truthfully, were you conscious of having these before I called them to your attention? Of course not. But when you had an earache, joint pain or a sore throat you were *very much* conscious of them. When parts of your body are healthy and functioning well, they are not in your awareness. This is also true of you *as a person*. If you are in good emotional health and are functioning well psychologically, you are not aware of *yourself*. If you did something that caused you embarrassment or someone humiliated you and your face turned red or pale, you would be acutely aware of yourself. This would likely be the case, should you make a mistake, even if no one was around. As with parts of the body, so with the whole person. *Being conscious of yourself for more than just a fleeting moment means that something may be wrong.*

An extreme example of this is a person who is paranoid. He thinks he is being followed and that everyone is staring at him. He may think his voice is being recorded and that pictures are being taken of him. This is a form of mental illness, and the consciousness of oneself is extreme. This is also true of the polar opposite. A person may feel that he is being totally ignored. No one is noticing his presence. No one is looking at him. It is as if he did not exist. This is a feeling of inferiority which is psychologically unhealthy, and again, is characterized by severe self-consciousness.

A person who is in good emotional health and thinks well of himself is not likely to be concerned whether or not people are looking at him. It makes no difference to him whether they notice him or not. On the other hand, people with feelings of inferiority may do things to attract attention. The more intense the feelings of inferiority, the more extreme are the attention-seeking mechanisms.

People who are confident of their ability to function do whatever they are doing with their full attention to the task at hand. People who are unsure of themselves may be concerned about possibly making a mistake and the impact and repercussions of their mistake. Instead of directing their full attention to what they are doing, they may interject themselves into the scene and may become distracted. Unfortunately, this very distraction may bring about the mistake they fear making.

When I did psychiatric evaluations for prison, a young man was brought for an examination. He had been arrested in a bungled bank robbery. His father was a self-made man who had gone from rags to riches by his hard work and business acumen. The son felt himself totally dwarfed by his father's success, and that he had very meager accomplishments of his own. When he entered the interview room, he smiled and said, "Hello, doctor. Did you see my picture on the front page of the newspaper today?" He had finally succeeded in calling attention to himself. The motive for the bank robbery may have been more for being noticed than for the money.

Do you remember the school clown, the kid who was forever getting kicked out of the class because of his antics? Do you remember how he smiled when the teacher made him leave the room? That was a smile of triumph. Thirty kids plus the teacher were all focusing on him! As I recall, the class clown was not a stupid kid. He could have achieved a positive recognition by excelling in his studies. But because he did not think he was bright enough to excel academically, he chose the negative road to prominence.

People who are not self-conscious have no need to draw attention to themselves. They generally do not think about themselves. The "self" takes care of itself "automatically."

There are two ways for a mechanism to operate: manual or automatic. When a machine runs on automatic, you leave it alone and it performs its function. On manual, however, you have to direct its function. Automatic is not only easier than manual, but it is also more efficient. On manual it is much more likely that one may make a mistake.

The human being operates on both levels. We do not think about our breathing. That runs automatically by one of the centers in the brain. Sure, we could take over and do our breathing on manual, thinking, "Inhale . . . now exhale. Inhale . . . now exhale." If you did that, you would not have your mind free to do anything else. Furthermore, the automatic control center knows when it is necessary to increase your respiration, such as when you exert yourself in order to bring more oxygen into the system. On manual, you would not know just how fast you should be breathing at any given time. Nature is wise. (The term "nature" refers to G-d acting through the apparent "laws of nature.") It delegated the breathing to the automatic control center.

This is also true of blinking, which is necessary to keep the cornea from drying out. Could you imagine what it would be like if you had to control your blinking consciously or if you had to think about walking?. "Lift the left foot and put it forward. Now bring the right foot forward and put it in front of the left foot." Not only would we not be able to do anything else, but we would probably go insane trying to control our breathing, blinking and walking.

So nature did the wise thing. It put those functions that are necessary for life under automatic control. We may at times take over for a short while and change the rate of our breathing or blinking, but for the greater part of our lives, these functions proceed automatically and efficiently.

Those functions that are not essential to preserve life and health are done manually. You do not write a letter or cook a roast automatically. You think about what to write or what ingredients to add. You look at the container to make sure it is onion powder and not cinnamon that you are putting on the meat you plan to roast. Nature assigned these to our conscious control. It trusted you to check the ingredients, because in the worst scenario, cinnamon on the roast is not tasty, but it is not fatal. But improper breathing can have very grave consequences, so nature put it under automatic control.

Here is more evidence of the superiority of automatic over manual function. Golf pros give lessons on how to play golf. They teach you how to grip the golf club, how to stand, where to keep your head during the swing and how far your right heel should be off the ground among other things. When you try to put all these teachings into action, you do not exactly come up with a stellar performance. Why? Because when you have to follow all those directions, you are on manual. Your swing has the grace of a mechanical tin soldier. The poise and graceful movements of the golf pros are due to the fact that they *don't* think about all these things. It comes naturally to them. They function on automatic. Of course, the more you practice what you have been taught, the more automatic your playing becomes and you can improve your score. But as long as you have to use manual, your score will suffer.

What abut the "self"? Except for special circumstances, such as making a *chesbon hanefesh* (personal accounting), the self should run on automatic, without your attention being directed toward it. That will allow you to function smoothly. If, for whatever reason, you take the self out of automatic and direct it manually, you will have the same inefficiency as if you controlled your breathing automatically.

Even if one cannot operate totally on automatic, there is great benefit in decreasing the degree of manual control. The less one does manually, the easier one's life can be.

Tactics for Use in Battling the *Yetzer Hara*

Just as the *yetzer hara* has developed new strategies, we can develop new defensive tactics.

First, let us realize that the older, time-proven methods are still of great value. They have not lost their efficacy. It is just that some have to be upgraded and reinforced.

The foremost antidote against the *yetzer hara* is the study of Torah. "I created the *yetzer hara,* and I created the Torah as its antidote" (*Kiddushin* 30b). However, as was noted earlier, this antidote requires the will that Torah should be effective in this way. Studying Torah as one would any other subject without the intention that it should help one become a better person is of little value.

In the prayer inaugurating the new month, we ask for a life of reverence for G-d and fear of sin. Fear of sin does not mean fear of punishment. Rather, it means fearing the harm that sin would do to us.

People often attribute sin to their inability to resist temptation, and place the blame on the *yetzer hara.* This is not quite right.

In an experimental laboratory, mice were placed at one

side of an electrical surface and various objects which they desired were placed at the other side. A mild electric current was then passed through the grid, which caused some pain to the mice if they ran across the grid. The mice would run for their desired objects, but when the current was increased to the point where the pain exceeded the desire, the mice would not cross the grid.

Simply at the biological level, if a person's awareness of the gravity of a sin exceeds the temptation, he will refrain from committing it.

Our concept of the gravity of violating halachah pales in comparison with that of previous generations. It can be seen as the polar opposite of what happened with smoking. Previous generations were not aware of the malignant effects of smoking. Now that we are aware of it, smoking has been banned in airplanes and in most public places. We know that not only is secondary smoke toxic, but hotels and car-rental agencies make nonsmoking rooms and cars available for those who wish to preserve their health. Only reckless people choose to ignore the facts and jeopardize their lives with cigarettes.

Similarly, previous generations were aware that violating Torah is malignant, and they took many precautions to protect their spiritual health. Today, even many people who observe Torah are not fully aware of the gravity of a transgression.

We can overcome the temptation of the *yetzer hara* by studying the Torah literature to further our awareness of the gravity of sin. Again, this does not refer to fear of punishment, but to the harm that sin can cause.

The *mussar* writings give a parable of a king who wanted to test the loyalty of his subjects. He engaged someone to circulate among the population and foment rebellion, pointing out the flaws in the kingdom and how life would be more pleasant under a different regime.

The man did as he was told. Some people who were suffering from chronic discontent fell prey to the man's promises of a better life after the revolution. The wiser among them were not duped. They said, "How can such a rebel function in a kingdom where the king could easily do away with him? His existence can only be because the king commissioned him to test our loyalty. I will have nothing to do with him." These wise people did not enter into an argument to defend the king. They simply turned a deaf ear to this man and ignored him.

This is true of the Satan/*yetzer hara*. When it tells us to do things that are in defiance of G-d's will, we should realize that G-d can easily do away with it. We should be wise enough to know that this is only to test our loyalty to G-d. There is no point in getting into a discussion or argument with the *yetzer hara*. We should simply ignore it and go about our business, doing what we are supposed to do.

> A chassid once asked the Rebbe of Rizhin if he could give him a rule of thumb to guide him in everyday life. The Rebbe responded, "Think of how a tightrope walker keeps his delicate balance. If he feels a slight tug to one side, he leans a bit to the opposite side.
>
> "Most of our drives," the Rebbe said, "emanate from our bodily desires, which are often the urgings of the yetzer hara. Therefore, when you have a desire to do something, do not immediately yield to the temptation. Pause for a moment and think why you should not do it. You may realize that it is not the right thing to do. Should you decide that it is proper, you will be in a better position to channel the urge so that you do it in a way which will be in the service of G-d.
>
> "Take hunger, for example. If you promptly succumb to the desire to eat a specific food, you may eat something which is unhealthy. Look for reasons why you should not eat it. This gives you the opportunity to

evaluate whether it is really good for you. If you decide it is healthy, you are then in a position to reflect, 'Eating this food will provide me with the energy I need to observe Torah and mitzvos.'"

This was an excellent instruction two hundred years ago and is still a valuable guideline. Incidentally, using this method in the example cited would help eliminate what doctors feel is a major threat to the health of millions of people: compulsive eating. Implementing the Rebbe's advice could lessen the compulsivity.

Sincere study of the *mussar* writings is a potent weapon against the *yetzer hara*. However, setting up a defense against an enemy attack and walking away from it leaves one very vulnerable. One must constantly check that the defensive system is intact. Any weak point in the system invites an attack by the enemy. This is equally true of defending oneself against the *yetzer hara*. Studying *Mesilas Yesharim* (*The Path of the Just*) one time and putting it away does not accomplish much. This book and other *mussar* writings should be studied and reviewed regularly. This defensive system cannot be neglected.

Many things can distort our thinking and result in improper judgments. If we are aware of this danger, we can look for ways to avert it,

I was once driving in the country when I ran into a very thick fog. Visibility was so limited that I could not see the taillights of the car in front of me. By the same token, I knew that the car behind me could not see me. I was in danger of colliding with both. If I stood still, I would be struck by the car behind me. If I tried to advance too fast, I would hit the car in front of me. I could not turn off the road, because I could not see what was at the side. Fortunately, out of the corner of the windshield I could make out the white line along the side of the road. If I kept the car parallel to the white line, I would not go off the road. I did that, inching along slowly until I was out of the fog.

Just as there is an external fog, there can be an internal fog when one's mind is clouded by a variety of desires and intentions. The works of *mussar* can be our "white line" which prevents us from going off the straight path.

An additional defensive technique can be acquired by observing the long lines that may stretch the length of a block when the lottery jackpot exceeds $100 million. Everyone in line has the hope that he will be the lucky one to become an instant multimillionaire. Perhaps a few may win the prize, perhaps only one of many millions may win and perhaps no one will win.

Just think of what would happen if a person would be assured that if he buys a ticket, he would win. Why, he would arise before dawn to be the first in line to buy a ticket. Only a fool would pass up such an opportunity for instant wealth.

R' Itzele of Petersburg points out that in the spiritual realm, there is one great advantage the *yetzer tov* has over the *yetzer hara*. Deterioration of behavior is generally not precipitous. If a person deviates from Torah observance, it is usually a gradual process, beginning with minor infractions and progressing to more serious ones. That is the way the *yetzer hara* operates.

However, the *yetzer tov* has a distinct advantage. A person who was totally dissolute can become a *tzaddik* in a fraction of a second. The Talmud states that if a man marries a woman on the condition that he is a perfect *tzaddik*, the marriage may be valid even if he was known to be profligate. Why? Because he might have had a momentary thought of sincere *teshuvah*, which could transform him from being a complete *rasha* (evil person) to a perfect *tzaddik* (*Kiddushin*; *Kochvei Ohr* p.44).

The Talmud cites a case of Elazar ben Doradia, who was thoroughly dissolute, but who had an abrupt change of heart and profoundly regretted his decadent behavior. A heavenly voice declared, "Rabbi Elazar ben Doradia is assured of heavenly reward in Gan Eden (Paradise)" (*Avodah Zarah* 17a).

Think of it! A person can be assured of winning a spiritual sweepstake and become a perfect *tzaddik* instantaneously! When we see people waiting in line for hours for even the most remote chance of becoming instantaneously wealthy, we should be stimulated to avail ourselves of the opportunity to become instant *tzaddikim*.

Although it was noted that Torah study in absence of proper *middos* is not meritorious, there is an exception to this. The Talmud says that a person should always learn Torah, even if he does not have the best intentions, because Torah study itself will elevate him (*Pesachim* 50b). This is not in conflict with the previous statement. The commentaries explain that if one lacks proper *middos* and studies Torah *with the hope that it will help him refine his middos*, it will indeed do so.

We have unprecedented opportunities to study Torah today. Not only have the Talmud and countless Torah writings been translated into English, but a variety of Torah lectures and inspirational messages are available on audiotapes and via telephone. One can listen to Torah tapes while driving. If a person listens with hope that the words of Torah will help refine one's *middos*, he will have dealt the *yetzer hara* a decisive blow.

Just as there are unprecedented opportunities for Torah study, there are also unlimited opportunities for acts of *tzedakah* and *chessed* (kindness). In the *shtetl*, one's avenues for doing *tzedakah* and *chessed* were rather limited to the population of the village or to occasional itinerants. Today, communications are such that we have far greater opportunities for *tzedakah* and *chessed*. We can donate across the continent and across the ocean via telephone using our credit card number.

We are often made aware of the plight of needy families

who live far from us. There are life-saving medical treatments that are very costly, and we are often asked to participate in funding them. There are campaigns for blood and marrow donations, the latter being one of the greatest mitzvos. The Talmud says that acts of *gemilas chasadim* are superior in merit even to *tzedakah*, because *tzedakah* is done with one's belongings, whereas as *gemilas chasadim* is done with one's very body (*Succah* 49b). Until our time, giving blood was the only way in which one could donate an actual part of one's body to save a life. A marrow donation fulfills this great act of *chessed*.

An important act of *chessed* is *nosei b'ol chavero* (to empathize and share in another person's burden), and to join in activities for the good of the *klal*. The Jews in the *shtetl* were rather isolated and did not have as many opportunities to do these acts of *chessed*.

The Rebbe of Lubavitch said, "We are told that we can cleave to G-d by emulating His attributes. Just as G-d is merciful, so should we be merciful, etc.

"But we also say of G-d that He resurrects the dead. How can we possibly emulate that attribute?"

The Rebbe explained, "If you a see a person who is dejected and who has lost the spirit of life, and you say or do something which lifts his spirits and restores his will to live, then you have emulated G-d in resurrecting the dead."

The new ways of performing the mitzvos of *tzedakah* and *chessed* are powerful new ways to defeat the *yetzer hara*.

Many of the *mussar* writings advise defeating the *yetzer hara* by turning its own tactics against it. For example, the *yetzer hara* may say, "Stay in bed a while longer. It's too early to get up for the *minyan* and *daf yomi*. Look! It's still dark outside. You can sleep a bit more." You should respond by saying to the *yetzer hara*, "How come you're up already? If it is not too early for you to fulfill your duty, then it's not too early for me to arise and fulfill my obligations."

Just as we are vulnerable to subliminal advertising, we are also impressionable and may be affected by subtleties.

The most popular timepieces today are digital. These differ from traditional timepieces in that they indicate only the present time. Earlier clocks had hands which indicated the present time, but on the clock face there were numbers that indicated the past hours and the hours yet to come. Traditional clocks showed the past and future as well as the present. Digital clocks ignore the past and future.

The Talmud states that the way to avoid transgressions is to think of the past and of the future. "Consider three things and you will not come into the grip of sin. Know whence you came, whither you are going and before Whom you will give justification and reckoning" (*Ethics of the Fathers* 3:1). We have a proud heritage which we should not reject, and we have the responsibility to assure that future generations remain loyal to Judaism.

The *yetzer hara* tells us to ignore the past and the future. Think only of the present moment. "Eat, drink and be merry, for tomorrow you die." It tells us that there is nothing of value in life except pleasure. Enjoy everything you can and pay no attention to the consequences of your actions. It is this philosophy that leads people into the "grip of sin." It is this neglect of the past and of the future that causes young people to go for the momentary "high" of dangerous drugs, giving no thought to their responsibility of their heritage or to their sabotaging their future. Today's generation lives by "digital clocks."

But we can turn this strategy against the *yetzer hara*. When we are tempted to do something, it may be a struggle to resist it, especially if it is something that will always be forbidden. I have found that if an alcoholic thinks, "I can never take a drink," he is likely to relapse. The thought of never being able to drink is too formidable. Instead, he is told, "Take one day at a time. You can manage to abstain from drinking today. That's all you have to do. What about tomorrow? That is not today's concern. There is nothing you can do today about tomorrow's drinking, so there is no point in thinking about it. Tomorrow you will have the opportunity to think about tomorrow."

One recovered alcoholic marked off each day on his pocket calendar. He was sober for over forty-two years. He died at age 83, and the night before his death he wrote into his calendar 15,684. He was sober for forty-two years because he took each day as the only day he had to be concerned about.

I am indebted to one of my clients for an explanation of a difficult passage in the Torah. The Patriarch Jacob had to wait seven years to marry Rachel, and the Torah tells, "They seemed to him a few days because of his love for her" (*Genesis* 29:20). The commentaries ask: This seems the reverse of what happens when a person is separated from a beloved, when each day appears to be an eternity. How can we say that seven years seemed to be just a few days? My client pointed out that the translation of the Hebrew *yamim achadim* as "a few days" is not quite accurate. A few days would be *yamim muatim*. *Yamim achadim* means "single days." The Torah tells us that Jacob was able to tolerate a separation of seven years because he took them as "single days," one day at time.

This teaching is of great importance. We need only focus on abstaining from something forbidden today. We have time to deal with tomorrow's challenge tomorrow. We can put the digital clock to constructive use.

The *yetzer hara* may say, "Look at all the wrongs you have done in the past. You are too far gone to be able to be spiritual and come close to G-d. And with your background, you will never be able to be observant for the long term." This is when we should turn his techniques against him. "Don't tell me about my past or the difficulties of the future. I have a digital clock. I am concerned only about the immediate present, and for the present I can behave as G-d wants me to."

Another effective anti-*yetzer hara* strategy is to make a preemptive strike. If the enemy attacks you on your territory, you are on the defensive. If you attack him on his territory, you put him on the defensive. It is well known that the best defense is an offense.

If you wait until the *yetzer hara* tempts you to do something forbidden, you are on the defensive. If you forgo some things that are permissible, you have brought the battle onto its territory, and the *yetzer hara* is put on the defensive.

R' Shneur Zalman said, "What is forbidden is, of course, prohibited. But much of what is permissible is unnecessary."

Judaism does not advocate asceticism, but does not condone indulgence. As Rambam says, the appropriate path is the median between two extremes.

It is possible to be technically observant of Torah and yet be a coarse person. Ramban explains the verse "You shall be holy" (*Leviticus* 19:2), as meaning that simply abstaining from what is forbidden is not enough to make a person holy and spiritual. One can indulge in permissible things and be a coarse person although one has not violated any Torah prohibitions.

My work with addiction has taught me much. A person who regularly uses alcohol or drugs to achieve a desired sensation never remains at a stable level. The body becomes accustomed to the dose consumed, and the latter no longer produces the desired sensation. One then increases the dose, with the development of a relentless progression.

This is equally true of any pleasure-seeking activity. If one lives for the pursuit of pleasure, there is no limit to what one will desire. Even permissible pleasures can fuel the fire of addiction.

This is indeed a greater concern for us today than for past generations. So much has been made available to us that is permissible. For example, I pointed out earlier that in the past, the foods that were available for Passover were rather simple. As a child, we had chicken, meat, nuts, borscht, potatoes and more potatoes. Oh, yes. We did have marmalade as a candy. Today? Just visit the Passover section of the supermarket. Chocolates of every kind, chewing gum, marshmallows and more varieties of candies than one can consume. Dairy products galore. Parve and dairy ice-cream. Soft drinks of every flavor. All kinds of cakes and cookies.

Passover is just an indication of what is now available to us all year round.

Where does one draw the line? What is the median between asceticism and indulgence that Rambam advocates? The answer for this is different for each individual, and can be attained only by sincere daily study of *mussar* writings and by having a relationship with a competent Torah scholar as a teacher and mentor.

We should realize that failure to refine our *middos* and doing things that are forbidden by Torah are simply beneath our dignity. We are too good to engage in improper behavior.

We care for things that are beautiful and valuable. We are not particularly cautious in caring for cheap earthenware, but we are careful not to allow fine crystal or silver utensils to be damaged. We cherish these, handle them with care and polish them so that they sparkle.

The Torah says, "You are children to G-d you shall not deface yourselves" (*Deuteronomy* 14:1). We are bearers of a Divine soul. There is G-dliness within each of us. We are far too precious and beautiful to permit ourselves to be damaged physically or spiritually. Just as we polish our silver and jewelry to maximize their beauty, we should polish our *middos* to enhance their beauty.

The Sages teach that when Hillel left the academy, his students asked where he was going. "To do a mitzvah,"

Hillel replied. "What kind of mitzvah?" they asked. "I am going to the bathhouse," Hillel said. "Why is that a mitzvah?" they asked. Hillel responded, "Have you not noticed how they wash the statues of the emperor to keep them clean? Inasmuch as man was created in the image of G-d, we should show our respect for the Divine image by keeping it clean" (Vayikra Rabbah 34).

Indeed, we should respect the body. But it is only a receptacle for the *neshamah*, which is really the likeness of G-d. How careful we must be to beautify the *neshamah* and protect it from being marred. Just as we would not allow anyone to damage any valuable and beautiful possession, we should be equally zealous to prevent the *yetzer hara* from detracting from our Divine beauty.

The *yetzer hara* can exploit our natural emotions. Going against a natural feeling may be a decisive blow to the *yetzer hara*.

R' Menachem Mendel of Kosov had adversaries from whom he suffered. One of these fell on bad times, and knowing that R' Menachem Mendel gave tzedakah lavishly, he appealed to him for help. R' Menachem Mendel gave him a handsome donation.

R' Menachem Mendel's wife was outraged. "After the distress he has caused you, he deserved nothing, and certainly not the large amount you gave him."

R' Menachem Mendel said, "You are not the first to tell me that. A few moments ago there was someone else who said the same thing, even more convincingly."

"Who was that?" his wife asked.

"The yetzer hara," R' Menachem Mendel said.

Doing *lifnim meshuras hadin* (more than is required by the letter of the law) is a preemptive strike.

When R' Zalman of Vilna was a child, he overheard a dialogue on the eve of Yom Kippur. One man had asked forgiveness from another man, and the latter replied, "According to halachah, I am not required to forgive you because you slandered me."

The young Zalman said to him, "The Talmud states that Jerusalem was destroyed because they decided disputes according to the law of Torah (Bava Metzia 30a). But how can it be that observing the law of Torah resulted in a punishment?

"I think," the child said, "that although the Israelites had committed grave sins, G-d was willing to forgive them and not enforce the letter of the law as long as they were willing to do lifnim meshuras hadin. But when litigants insisted on enforcing the letter of the law, G-d acted toward them in the same manner. The letter of the law demanded that they be punished for their sins.

"It is now before Yom Kippur. You may invoke the law and refuse to forgive that man. But remember, when you ask forgiveness for your sins, G-d may treat you as you treat him."

With tears in his eyes, the man hugged young Zalman, and promptly told his offender that he forgived him wholeheartedly (Lekach Tov, Deuteronomy vol. 1 p. 106).

The Torah says, "Beware and guard yourself carefully, lest you forget the things that your eyes have seen and lest they stray from your heart . . . the day you stood before your G-d at Sinai" (*Deuteronomy* 4:9-10). R' Shlomo Wolbe suggests using imagery. Close your eyes and create the scene in your mind of several million men, women and children gathered at the foot of Sinai, which is afire with a heavenly flame and covered with clouds. The sound of the shofar grows louder and louder, and you feel the earth beneath you trembling. Only Moses has ascended the fiery mountain, and you hear the voice of G-d saying, "I am the Lord your G-d Who has delivered you from Egypt from the house of bondage."

Imagining this scene strengthens one's resolve to obey the Divine will (*Alei Shur* vol.1 p 46).

A recent finding by research psychologists has again shown the Talmudic teaching to be correct: "Delve in it (the Torah) and continue to delve in it, for everything is in it" (*Ethics of the Fathers* 5:26).

These psychologists studied families in which there were children with social problems: alcohol, drugs, violence, truancy, etc. They listed all the factors that they could find in these families. They did the same with families where there were no significant problems with the children. They fed all the data into computers to see whether there were any outstanding features that characterized the healthy families as compared to the problem-ridden families.

The most salient feature that distinguished the healthy families was *that the families ate their meals together!*

In the 14th century, Rabbeinu Asher (Rosh) wrote, "Set aside time before meals and before bedtime, *and discuss Torah at meals*" (*Orchos Chaim* 44).

R" Daniel Movshovitz expanded on this theme. "I have seen Torah scholars discuss Torah topics and refinement of *middos* with their families at mealtime." The Talmud says that sharing food is a powerful bonding force (*Sanhedrin* 103b). Utilizing mealtime to discuss Torah is most praiseworthy (*Ethics of the Fathers* 3:4), and it can have a very positive influence on children (*Lekach Tov, Deuteronomy* vol. 1 p.101).

An additional technique against the *yetzer hara* can be learned from the Midrash which states that when Jews embrace the mitzvos lovingly, Satan ceases to bring charges against them.

The commentaries cite the Talmud that when a person does *teshuvah* out of deep love for G-d and sincere regret for having disobeyed him, the sins he had done are not only forgiven but are transformed into merits (*Yoma* 86b). Therefore, if a person has done *teshuvah* out of love for G-d, enumerating the sins he did would be counterproductive for Satan, since it would only add to the person's merits.

If a person sincerely regrets his sins, the *yetzer hara* will desist from tempting him to sin, since his sins are likely to be transformed into merits.

I can understand this Midrash from my work with alcoholics. I have repeatedly observed that people who are diligent and sincere in achieving spirituality in their recovery develop exemplary personalities. Many times these people have said, "When I first came to terms with my alcoholism, I was deeply grieved over what I had done to myself and others. But now I can say that without recovery from alcoholism, I never could have become the person I am now. I am now actually grateful that I was alcoholic, because my recovery has brought me to a level of spirituality which I never would have reached otherwise."

There is no doubt that this is the intent of the Talmudic statement that the place occupied by a sincere *baal teshuvah* is superior to that of someone who was always a *tzaddik* (*Berachos* 34b).

An important tactic against the *yetzer hara* is to avoid procrastination when the opportunity to do a mitzvah presents itself. The *yetzer hara* can come up with ingenious reasons why not to do the mitzvah, even to the point that doing this mitzvah will result in the loss of opportunity to do other mitzvos.

R' Eliyahu Lopian cites the verse in the Torah that G-d loved the Patriarch Abraham because he was the one who would transmit G-d's teachings to future generations (*Genesis* 18:19). When G-d told Abraham to sacrifice Isaac, Abraham could have thought, "If Isaac is sacrificed, what will happen with my mitzvah to transmit G-d's teachings to future generations? Surely, I must have misunderstood what G-d said. He could not want me to lose the mitzvah of transmitting His ways to future generations." But Abraham did not make such calculations.

He heard the Divine commandment and arose "early in the morning" to carry it out without delay (*Genesis* 22:3).

Another weapon against the *yetzer hara* is to be scrupulously honest in money matters. Far be it for any Torah-observant person to commit theft. However, there may be breaches of fairness which people may ignore.

It is related that the Chafetz Chaim was traveling by train, and when the conductor collected the tickets, the Chafetz Chaim handed him two tickets. "Why are you giving me two tickets?" the conductor asked.

The Chafetz Chaim said, "The regulations are that a passenger is permitted only a certain quantity of baggage. I think my baggage exceeded that limit, so I bought a second ticket" (Darchei Mussar).

The Chafetz Chaim's total devotion to Torah study is legendary. Yet, he personally leafed through every book he sold to make sure that there was no missing or defective page. Just think of how much Torah he could have studied during this time! But his priority was that avoiding giving someone defective merchandise took precedence even over Torah study.

The Chafetz Chaim's son, R' Leib, writes that his father spent weeks in Warsaw at the printer, personally supervising the printing lest there be any defect, which he felt would constitute theft.

When R' Leib moved to Warsaw, the Chafetz Chaim turned over the supervision to him. One day the Chafetz Chaim received a letter from a man who had purchased the Mishnah Berurah,and several pages had been bound upside down. The Chafetz Chaim was beside himself, and promptly wrote to R' Leib, "My son, what have you done to me? All my life I tried to avoid the slightest trace of dishonesty, and now, due to your negligence, I have turned into a common thief!" The Chafetz Chaim immediately ordered a reprinting, and put ads in the newspapers that anyone finding a volume with the upside-down pages should return it for a replacement (Ateres L'Melech p. 107).

The yetzer hara is not stupid. It knows that with someone of this caliber it would be a waste of time to try and seduce him to sin.

R' Moshe Schreiber (Chasam Sofer) writes, "All my life I have worried about fulfilling the commandment, 'You shall be vindicated from G-d and from Israel' (*Numbers* 32:22). It is much easier to fulfill one's obligations to G-d than to one's fellow. The punishment for dereliction toward one's fellow is far, far greater than if one is derelict in mitzvos between man and G-d" (*Teshuvos Chasam Sofer* 59).

The late Torah scholar, R' Avraham Pam, writes, "In these days there are many people who are meticulous in observance of those mitzvos that are between man and G-d, but are not as careful in matters of money. This causes a frightening *chilul Hashem* (profaning the Divine Name;)" (*Atarah LaMelech* 113).

Exercising extra caution to achieve absolute honesty is an effective defense against the *yetzer hara.*

Shabbos as an Anti-*Yetzer Hara* Weapon

Shabbos is a precious gift which G-d gave to Israel. "I have a wonderful gift in My treasure stores," G-d said. "Its name is Shabbos. Tell the Children of Israel that I wish to give it to them" (*Shabbos* 10b).

A precious gift, indeed. "If a person observes Shabbos properly, all his sins are forgiven" (*Shabbos* 118b). If Shabbos can eradicate all one's sins, it certainly can help prevent them.

However, the Talmud qualifies this statement with the term "properly." Proper observance of Shabbos is more than abstaining from the restricted activities.

> *"If you restrain your foot, because of Shabbos; refrain from accomplishing your own needs on My holy day; if you proclaim Shabbos a delight, the holy and honored [day] of G-d, and you honor it by not engaging in your own affairs, from seeking your needs or discussing the forbidden. Then you shall delight in G-d and I shall mount you astride the heights of the world, and provide you the heritage of your forefather Jacob for the mouth of G-d has spoken" (Isaiah 58:13-14).*

Shabbos is referred to as a bride, *Lecha dodi likras kallah* (Come, my beloved, let us greet the bride). Shabbos is also referred to as *Shabbos malkesa*, the queen Shabbos. We should relate to Shabbos with affection as for a bride and with reverence as for a majestic queen.

In chassidic teaching, Shabbos dominates the entire week. Beginning on Wednesday, we should prepare ourselves for greeting the queen-bride of the forthcoming Shabbos, and the glow of the past Shabbos should linger on through Tuesday.

In contrast to the weekdays which are occupied primarily with work and other mundane activities, Shabbos should be a day of spirituality. On Shabbos we receive a *neshamah yeseirah*, an additional Divine spirit, which should elevate us above earthly matters. As a day of rest and celebration, we have festive meals and we may nap, but all other time should be devoted to some aspect of prayer and Torah study. Reading newspapers, secular magazines and books does not contribute anything toward spirituality and should be avoided.

The queen-bride Shabbos loves Torah and prayer. She loves to be honored with a festive meal. But think about how a bride would feel if the bridegroom paid her no attention and entertained himself by reading a magazine, a novel or studying for an exam. How painful she would feel to be so shunned! And such behavior in the presence of a queen would be considered a grave affront against the crown.

When we read about how the *tzaddikim* of previous generations revered and honored Shabbos, we may say, "That is indeed wonderful, but we cannot compare ourselves to those highly spiritual people." But listen to what the Talmud says about people who were not the least bit spiritual.

The Talmud says that there are people who are not trustworthy, and if they say that a questionable product is kosher, one may not rely on them. However, the same person who is suspect of lying and saying that a nonkosher food is kosher *may be relied upon with regard to certain products, if he says on Shabbos that they are acceptable.* Why? Because even an uncouth person is afraid to lie on Shabbos (*Jerusalem Talmud, Demai* 4:1).

Think of it! Here we have a person who may knowingly mislead a person and cause him to eat nonkosher food, yet on Shabbos he is reliable because his reverence for Shabbos would not allow him to lie. How many people can claim that they are much more truthful on Shabbos than during the week?

It is traditional that on Shabbos the father reviews with his children what they have learned during the week. Even young children who may spend much of the day playing come to know that Shabbos is a spiritual day.

Properly observed, Shabbos is a day of delight. The Midrash states that when we inaugurate Shabbos by reciting the last paragraph of the verses depicting creation (*Genesis* 2:1-3), which states that when Shabbos entered, G-d had completed all the work of creation, we, too, should feel on Friday evening that everything in the workweek has been completed. There is no carry over onto Shabbos. We do not owe any money, we do not have any uncollected debts, we are not concerned about whether we will be awarded a lucrative contract, whether the automobile is repairable, whether the bid we submitted for a house will be accepted or any of the myriad concerns that occur in the workweek.

The workweek often provides many causes for worry. On Shabbos we should be free of these. Listen to the prescription the great physician, Rambam, prescribed for elimination of worry.

> Take the roots of Shabbos, the cores of praise, gratitude, joy and trust and remove the seeds of anguish and worry. Take the blossoms of wisdom and

understanding and the roots of patience and content-ment and grind them in the mortar of meekness, and cook them all in the vessels of humility. Knead them with the sweetness of words and stir everything with the waters of grace and kindness. Give one who is sick with the illness of despair two spoonfuls morning and evening, together with three spoonfuls of the waters of clarity. Purify everything from the dross of anger and impatience, and mix everything in the essence of acceptance of the will of G-d, Master of praise and thankfulness, and have him drink it in vessels of Divine praise. The sick person will relax and be serene (Introduction to *Sefer HaNimtza*).

Sins are forgiven and erased when a person does *teshuvah* and resolves to improve his behavior. The reason that a person who observes Shabbos properly is forgiven for all his sins is because truly proper observance of Shabbos elevates one to a level where sinful behavior is unlikely to recur, and this constitutes *teshuvah*. This spiritual achievement also militates against all improper behavior and is, therefore, a powerful weapon against the *yetzer hara*.

Passover as an Anti-*Yetzer Hara* Weapon

Just as a comprehensive observance of Shabbos militates against the *yetzer hara,* so does observance of Passover.

The *mussar* works state that *chometz* is symbolic of the *yetzer hara*, and that the elimination of all *chometz* on the festival of liberation represents divesting oneself of all vestiges of the *yetzer hara.*

The restriction of *chometz* is different than that of other forbidden foods. While it is inappropriate to own nonkosher food, there is no biblical restriction against this. The restriction against *chometz,* however, is not only against eating it on Passover, but also against possessing it. Secondly, if a nonkosher food item is accidentally included in a kosher preparation, and the proportion of kosher to non-kosher is greater than sixty to one, the kosher preparation does not become *tereifah* (forbidden). On the other hand, if the tiniest morsel of *chometz* falls into a huge vat of kosher food, and the proportion is many millions to one, the entire vat is rendered forbidden.

Why is the restriction of *chometz* so severe?

Matzah is the "bread of freedom." *Chometz* is the antithesis of matzah. The message is that we should value freedom so greatly that we should not allow even the slightest incursion against it.

Chometz differs from other forbidden foods. *Tereifah* cannot transform other foods. A small piece of *tereifah* food that is overwhelmed by a much greater quantity of kosher food may be considered negligible. A tiny fragment of *chometz*, however, can transform a huge quantity of dough to become *chometz* like itself. In other words, *chometz* is of an "infectious" nature.

The *yetzer hara*, too, is of an infectious nature. It is insatiable and seeks to transform a person into a totally self-centered creature, striving for nothing other than self-gratification.

Passover is much more than an "Independence Day" celebration. The latter is celebrated with a day of parades, picnics, fireworks and patriotic speeches. Rendering the house surgically clean of *chometz* and living under rigid restrictions for an entire week is not the way one celebrates an Independence Day.

In the Haggadah *From Bondage to Freedom*, I related that a young man who had recovered from a severe heroin addiction returned home for Passover. When his father began reciting the Haggadah passage, "We were slaves . . . ," he interrupted him. "Father," he said, "can you truthfully say that *you* were a slave? *I* can tell you what it means to be a slave. When I was addicted to heroin, I had no freedom of choice. I did whatever was necessary to procure the drug. I did things that I could never have imagined I was capable of doing, because the drug was my taskmaster. I had to do whatever it dictated. Today I am free. Today I can make choices."

This made me aware of what Passover was all about. Historically, we were slaves to Pharaoh in Egypt. But a person can be a slave to internal compulsions, which do not allow him freedom of choice. Many people who love life and wish to have good health are unable to stop the deadly habit of cigarette smoking. They are every bit as enslaved by tobacco as our ancestors were by Pharaoh. This is equally true of any compulsion, whether it be compulsive eating, compulsive gambling, or compulsive pursuit of acclaim or wealth. Anyone subject to a compulsion of any nature is not free.

Animals are not free. They are under the dictatorship of their bodies. Whatever the body craves, the animal must do. It cannot defy a bodily desire.

The primary distinction between man and animals is that a human being is free to make choices. He can defy a bodily urge because of ethical and moral considerations.

Surrendering the right to freedom of choice and subjecting oneself to complying with physical desires is essentially abdicating the most important feature of humanness.

The message of Passover is that G-d delivered us from slavery in order that we be truly free, free of internal as well as external domination.

As noted, the *yetzer hara* is as infectious as *chometz.* It can insidiously creep up on a person and progressively bring more of one's behavior under its control.

There are the essentials of life and there are conveniences and luxuries. One of the tactics of the *yetzer hara* is to habituate us to conveniences and luxuries so that they become necessities.

For example, the first automobile I owned a half century ago had neither power steering nor air-conditioning. Inasmuch as these were extremely rare then, I was perfectly satisfied with my vehicle. Today I would not think of having a car that is not air conditioned or that lacked power steering. What were once conveniences have now become necessities.

Everyone can find similar situations in their own lives where one feels deprived without things that were at one time considered luxuries. We have to admit that if we could be satisfied with what are truly the basic essentials of life, we would have much more time to devote to spiritual pursuits. Many of us are driven to invest more time and effort in order to enjoy conveniences which have now become necessities. We are no longer free to utilize our time and energies for what is truly important. The *yetzer hara* has succeeded in enslaving us.

My mother used to relate the comment of a philosopher who, upon seeing a display in a store window, said, "I never knew before that there are so many things that I could do without."

This is no doubt that this is the meaning of the Talmudical statement, "Eat bread with salt, drink water in small measure, sleep on the ground, and live a life of deprivation. If you do this, you are praiseworthy, and all is well with you. You are praiseworthy in this world and all is well with you in the World to Come" (*Ethics of the Fathers* 6:4). If one can accept living with just the bare necessities, then one's life does not become an endless pursuit of comforts, and if one does attain some of the luxuries of life, they do not spur him on to the bottomless pit of self-gratification. The pleasantries of life can be enjoyed without their becoming infectious.

But the *yetzer hara* seeks to divert people from this Talmudical teaching. By making the conveniences of life necessities, it *compels* one to seek them, and whenever we are compelled, we lose some of our precious freedom. If we fully appreciated the message of Passover and realized that the infectious nature of *chometz* is the antithesis of freedom, we would understand why every tiny fragment of *chometz* is forbidden on the festival on which we celebrate our liberation from enslavement, We would guard our freedom zealously and refuse to be enslaved by the drives for self-gratification.

This does not mean that we should deny ourselves the pleasantries of life. Rather, that we be cautious that we be master over the things we enjoy and not allow them to be master over us.

Just as we should zealously protect our own freedom, we should be equally cautious not to encroach on the freedom of other people. As spouses, parents, employers, or in other relationships where we may feel we have authority, we must be most careful not to deprive other people of their right to free choice. This is what the Talmud meant, "Let the dignity of your fellow be as dear to you as your own," (*Ethics of the Fathers* 2:15). Teachers are in a position of authority over their students, and must avoid abusing it.

> *The great sage, R' Isser Zalman Meltzer, was testing several young yeshivah students on their Talmud studies. One boy gave a totally incorrect interpretation to a Talmudic passage. The sage tried to politely correct him by saying, "I'm sure what you really meant was this." But the young boy refused to be corrected, insisting his interpretation was right. After several attempts at correcting the youngster without embarrassing him failed, R' Isser Zalman arose and went into an adjacent room. He was seen to be pacing to and fro, repeating to himself, "Respecting the dignity of others applies to children as well as to grown-ups."*

A number of Torah commentaries say that the phrase, "Man was created in the likeness of G-d" (*Genesis* 1:27), means that man, like G-d, has freedom of choice. Animals are totally dominated by their bodies, and angels, while being spiritual beings, are emissaries of G-d and must carry out His will. Man alone is free to choose his actions. We should value our freedom not only because it dignifies us as humans, but also because it elevates us to the lofty status of being like G-d. The *yetzer hara* wishes to deprive us of this uniqueness. A profound understanding of the meaning of Passover can help us thwart the *yetzer hara's* scheme.

Applying What We Have Learned

I t has been disturbing, to say the least, to see that some people who have studied *mussar* seem to have been unaffected by it. The teachings of *mussar* seem to have failed to penetrate their thoughts and feelings.

I believe this is due to the failure of truly incorporating the words we so often say in our prayers, that Torah is our very life. Unless we truly believe that Torah teachings are as vital to our spiritual lives as oxygen is to our physical lives, we are not likely to be sufficiently affected by *mussar.*

R'Avraham Pam cites the Talmudic ruling that if a person sees a friend who needs help to unload a burden from his mule, and an adversary who needs help putting a load on his mule, he should help his adversary first, even though unloading the friend's mule would be relieving the animal. Why? Because by helping someone whom he dislikes, he is subduing his *yetzer hara* (*Bava Metzia* 32b).

R' Pam asks: Does not learning *mussar* result in subduing the *yetzer hara?* He answers that the sages of the Talmud knew that book learning is not enough to uproot the dislike of another person. It requires action, doing a favor for him to overcome the enmity (*Atareh LaMelech* p. 86).

I must draw here on my experience in treating alcoholism.

There are numerous places where the prophets rebuke the people by comparing their behavior to that of drunkards. If errant spiritual behavior is similar to that of the alcoholic, then perhaps we may learn how to correct our behavior and our propensity to yield to the *yetzer hara* by observing how an alcoholic overcomes his craving for alcohol.

I had one client who was given a final warning at work that one more drinking episode would result in termination of his job. The awareness that he might lose his livelihood made him take his recovery very seriously. He was told to avoid even the slightest amount of alcohol, because it would trigger a binge.

One day I received an emergency call from him. He had been invited to a friend's party, and although he avoided alcohol, he did drink some punch. The first sip told him that the punch had been "spiked" with alcohol. He promptly ran to the phone and called me. "I accidentally swallowed some alcohol," he said in a voice of panic. "What should I do? I'm afraid I won't be able to control myself. If I drink again I will lose my job. Should I go into the hospital for a few days?" I gave the man the necessary instructions which helped prevent a relapse.

Let me present a different case. A person buys a candy bar which he knows has a *hechsher* (kosher approval). After eating it, he notices that the kosher symbol is not on the wrapper, and concludes that this was removed because this candy now contains a nonkosher ingredient. He certainly feels badly that he may have eaten *tereifah* (nonkosher), and his reaction is likely to be, "I must be more careful in the future. I will check to make sure that the kosher symbol is present before I eat something."

But do we not learn in the Talmud that "sin begets sin"

(*Ethics of the Fathers* 4:2)? Even an inadvertent sin may lead to another sin, just as an inadvertent swallow of alcohol may lead to a binge. Why does this man not run to a phone and call his rabbi, saying, "What should I do? I may have inadvertently eaten *tereifah*. How can I prevent this from causing further sins?"

The difference between the two cases is that for the alcoholic, "one drink will lead to another," is not simply intellectual knowledge. Experience has proven this to be an undeniable fact. He does not just *know* this to be true. He *feels* it to be true. The man with the candy bar, although he is committed to observing kosher, does not have a similar deep conviction that "sin begets sin."

In medicine we know that if an antibiotic or disinfectant kills millions of germs but leaves one bacteria untouched, that is enough to cause a severe infection. This is what a truly Torah-observant person must feel. Any infraction of halachah, even if one thinks it to be minor, is enough to set into motion a deteriorating course.

In the treatment field there is a truism that an alcoholic does not recover until he has reached "rock bottom;" i.e., until he has an emotional awareness that alcohol is deadly for him. If we would have an emotional conviction that Torah is our very life and that the slightest deviation from Torah can be deadly to our spiritual life, we would incorporate the teachings of *mussar* in our behavior.

Interestingly, the teachings of the Talmud and *mussar* bear some similarity to the steps an alcoholic must take to recover. The Talmud says that the *yetzer hara* renews itself, grows in strength every day and wishes to destroy a person, and that without the help of G-d a person could not withstand it (*Kiddushin* 30b, *Succah* 52a). It also says that one does not commit a sin unless one is overtaken by an insane idea (*Sotah* 3a). Every person wants to live, and intellectually one knows that yielding to the *yetzer hara* can be deadly. Sin can occur only because the *yetzer hara* deludes a person into denying this. Every sin is, therefore, the result of a delusion, and all sin is indeed insanity.

The first step an alcoholic must take in recovery is to recognize that he is powerless over alcohol and that only a power greater than himself can save him from the insanity of drinking. Similarly, the first step a person must take in the battle with the *yetzer hara* is to recognize that yielding to it is insanity, and that only with the help of G-d can one withstand the delusion of the *yetzer hara*.

The next step in recovery is to make a fearless inventory and to share it with another person. The *mussar* writings are replete with the necessity of frequently making a *cheshbon hanefesh* (spiritual accounting). R' Shlomo Wolbe says that one should do this in writing, and should carry a notebook in which he can write down the various manifestations of his *middos*. R' Elimelech of Lizhensk says that one should acquire a trusted friend before whom one can reveal all of one's actions and thoughts.

Once a person has made a moral inventory and is aware of his character defects, he must do everything within his power to correct them, and then pray for G-d to help him eliminate them. I related earlier that the Chafetz Chaim used to pray fervently that G-d remove his feelings of anger. He knew that he could control his reactions to provocation, but that eliminating the *feeling* of anger was beyond his control. He, therefore, prayed to G-d to help him with what was beyond his own means.

The next step in recovery is that one must make a list of all those he had harmed and, wherever possible, make amends to them.

The Talmud says, "If the spirit of one's fellows is not pleased with him, the spirit of G-d is not pleased with him" (*Ethics of the Fathers* 3:13). A person who antagonizes others does not incur G-d's favor.

The Talmud says, "Sins committed against another person are not atoned for by Yom Kippur until one has placated the offended person" (*Yoma* 85b). If one has harmed or offended someone, *teshuvah* is ineffective until one has made necessary restitution and has attained that person's forgiveness. R' Dessler cites the kabbalist, R' Moshe of Cordova, who says that failure to seek the forgiveness of the offended person renders the *teshuvah* that one has done for all other sins ineffective (*Michtav M'Eliyahu*). The *mussar* writings repeatedly emphasize the Talmudic principle that "Love your fellow person as yourself" is the fundamental principle of Torah.

Similarly, one must be forgiving of others. The Baal Shem Tov cited the verse, "G-d is your shadow" (*Psalms* 121:5), and explained that just as a shadow mimics one's movements, so does G-d act toward a person the way one acts toward others. If one easily forgives those who offend him, then he merits forgiveness from G-d.

The next step in recovery is to continue taking a moral inventory, and when wrong, *promptly* admit it. Making a *cheshbon hanefesh* once or even several times is not adequate. We must continually take stock of ourselves. Remember the words of Rabbeinu Bachya, that the *yetzer hara* is never asleep on the job. "You may be asleep, but the *yetzer hara* is always alert."

Upon discovering that one has done something improper, one should *promptly* admit it. One cannot rectify a misdeed unless one acknowledges having done it. The natural tendency is to justify one's mistakes, as Solomon says, "All of a person's ways are right in his own eyes" (*Proverbs* 16:2). We must be extremely vigilant of the tactic of the *yetzer hara* to blind us to our mistakes and character defects.

The Talmud notes that King Saul committed only one sin but was not forgiven, whereas King David sinned twice and was forgiven (*Yoma* 22b). When the prophet Samuel reprimanded Saul for not fulfilling the Divine command, Saul tried to justify his actions and only later admitted that he was wrong (*I Samuel* 15:13-24). When the prophet Nathan reprimanded David, he immediately said, "I have sinned" (*II Samuel* 12:13). Proper *teshuvah* requires *prompt* admission of one's sin.

Inasmuch as the principles of recovery are so similar to the teachings of *mussar*, how did secular alcoholics discover them? The answer is quite simple.

The Talmud states that if the Torah had not been given to us, we would have been obligated to learn rules of proper behavior from observation of nature. For example, observation of ants can teach respect for private property. If an ant has procured a piece of grain, no other ant will touch it. Similarly, we could have learned fidelity from doves, who are monogamous (*Eruvin* 100a).

One might ask: Without Torah as a guide, who is to say that man would have made these observations? Perhaps he would have learned rapaciousness from tigers and promiscuity from dogs.

Solomon says that G-d created man straight and simple, but man sought to complicate things with his calculations (*Ecclesiastes* 7:29). Man's pristine nature would have led him to make the correct observations to learn proper moral and ethical behavior. If man does not do so, it is because his judgment is subject to the influence and temptations of the *yetzer hara*, which seeks gratification of all physical drives.

The alcoholic tries to assuage his discomfort and achieve self-gratification by drinking. When the drinking results in a painful, rock-bottom crisis, he realizes he must give up the pursuit of self-gratification. Bitter experience has shown him that this is self-defeating and devastating. Once the primacy of seeking self-gratification is overcome, he is then able to embark on a course of searching for meaning in life. This is why spiritual progress is an essential for recovery. It is the pursuit of spirituality that led people to the formulation of the steps for recovery.

Many people do not reach a rock-bottom crisis. There are the ups and downs in life, and indeed, some people experience much distress. The embodiment of *mussar* is not contingent on suffering. It requires a realization of the utter nothingness and meaninglessness of life if one does not have a goal beyond the pursuit of pleasure and avoidance of discomfort.

R' Yerucham Levovitz points out that the psalms are replete with King David's pleas that G-d save him from the depths of Gehinnom. The *tzaddikim* of yore knew just what was meant by "the imagery of man's heart is evil from his youth" (*Genesis* 8:21), and they had a dread of being misled by the evil inclination within them. The mere possibility of sin was a "rock-bottom" feeling, which enabled them to take the necessary and even drastic steps to avoid it (*Daas Chochmah U'Mussar* vol.6 p.20).

We think of people who are motivated to perform mitzvos by the reward of *Gan Eden* (Paradise) as being pious. They are indeed praiseworthy, but the Talmud de-emphasizes serving G-d out of anticipation for reward, even a heavenly reward (*Ethics of the Fathers* 1:3). The true motivation for Torah observance should be the realization that it is the only way one can achieve a relationship with G-d. One must feel, at the deepest emotional level, that life without closeness to G-d is intolerable.

It is related that R' Shneur Zalman was once heard crying out, "I do not want Your *Gan Eden!* I do not want Your *Olam Haba* (reward in the Eternal World)! I want only You!"

King David says, "I search for You, my G-d. My soul thirsts for You; my flesh pines for You, as when one is in an arid desert, exhausted and without water" (*Psalms* 63:2). When the craving for G-d is as intense as is the desire of a person in the desert for water, whose throat is parched and who feels he cannot live a moment longer without water, then one is ready to incorporate the teachings of *mussar* that will bring one closer to G-d.

The chassidic master, the Shpoler Zeide, pleaded in defense of Israel; "Master of the Universe! You have put the terror of Gehinnom in the *Reishis Chochmah* (a classic work of *mussar*), and You have placed the objects that can gratify one's desires before people's eyes. How can You expect them to make the right choice? If You had put the terror of Gehinnom before people's eyes, and the objects of temptation in the books, people would choose properly."

True, G-d is an abstraction, not accessible to the senses. We cannot see, touch or hear him. The objects of our desires are very much subject to our senses. However, if we overcome our indolence and put our minds to work in a sincere search for truth, the belief in G-d can outweigh what we experience with our senses.

R' Mendel of Kotzk said, "Some *tzaddikim* have seen the *Ushpizin* (the seven Patriarchs) in the succah. I have never seen them, but I believe they are there. Believing is superior to seeing them."

If we will develop a profound *emunah* (faith) and feel the utter desperation of what life would be like without closeness to G-d, we will be ready to apply the teachings of *mussar*, and move them from an intellectual understanding to an emotional experience.

Alas! Sometimes our service of G-d is not even a full intellectual experience, but merely something we do out of habit. R' Chaim Shmulevitz devotes two essays to "The Danger of Habit" and "The Anesthesia of Habit" (*Sichos Mussar* 5731:16, 32). This is hardly a new problem. We find the prophet Isaiah complaining that people were worshiping G-d as a matter of rote rather than devotion (*Isaiah* 29:13). Unfortunately, even the study of *mussar* can be rendered ineffective if it, too, becomes a matter of rote.

R' Shmulevitz cites a Midrash (Bereishis Rabbah 65:62) to point out the potency of an intense emotional experience. Yakum of Tzrororos had defected to the Romans. On Shabbos, his uncle, the great sage Yose ben Yoezer, was led on horseback to his execution. The nephew mocked his uncle, "Look at the horse your Master has provided for you and look at the horse my masters have given me!" The sage responded, "If those who defy G-d are so richly rewarded, just think of how those who serve Him are rewarded."

The nephew said, "Was there anyone who served G-d with greater devotion than you did?" The sage responded, "And if those who served G-d are never-theless punished for their transgressions, just think of the punishment that awaits those who defy Him."

The impact of the sage's words shocked Yakum "like the venom of a viper." He held court on himself, and judged himself deserving of the death penalty for his violations of Torah. He pronounced a death sentence on himself and killed himself.

Yose ben Yoezer said of his nephew's intense and radical teshuvah, "In just a matter of moments he preceded me into Gan Eden (Paradise)."

R' Shmulevitz points out that an intense emotional exper-ience of *teshuvah* can cause so complete a transformation of one's character that a person who had repudiated Judaism and collaborated with the Romans merited Gan Eden.

If an emotional experience can elevate a heretic and sinner to so lofty a spiritual status, just think of the spiritual heights someone observant of Torah could attain if his devotion to Torah was emotional as well as intellectual.

If we were not victims of habit, we would see everything in nature as a miracle. A tiny seed is buried in the ground, disintegrates and produces a tree which will bear beautiful blossoms and produce many thousands of delicious fruit for years. Is this any less of a miracle just because it happens so often? We are the beneficiaries of many miracles every day of our lives, as we say three times daily in the *Amidah*, thanking G-d "for Your miracles which are daily with us." Yes, we say it, but the words lack feeling. As the Talmud says, "The beneficiary of a miracle does not recognize it as such" (*Niddah* 31a). If our senses were not, as R' Shmulevitz says, "anesthetized" by habit, we would have an emotional awareness of G-d.

One of the most effective ways of moving from an intellectual to an emotional grasp of spirituality is studying the lives of our great Torah personalities. We are fortunate in having biographies of these spiritual giants. One cannot read about R' Chaim Ozer Grodzinski, the Gerer Rebbe, the Steipler, R' Shlomo Zalman Auerbach and other great Torah personalities, many of whom we were fortunate to know, and remain phlegmatic.

The Torah says that we are to love G-d "and cleave unto him" (*Deuteronomy* 30:20). How can a mortal cleave unto G-d, Who is an all-consuming fire? The Talmud answers, "Cleave unto Torah scholars, and you will be cleaving unto G-d" (*Rashi, Deuteronomy* 11:22). Our *tzaddikim* serve G-d with a fiery passion, and we can absorb this passion if we are in their presence.

The Midrash says, "The accounts given by the servants of the Patriarch surpass even the Torah scholarship of their descendants" (*Bereishis Rabbah* 60:11). This is because Torah study may remain an intellectual exercise, whereas the actions and life styles of the Torah personalities translate the intellectual concepts into living deeds, which can stimulate an emotional experience and understanding.

Epilogue

The tactic most frequently used by the *yetzer hara* is *delusion*. It tries to convince an individual that wrong is right and that false is true. Even when it appears that it is using temptation, that, too, is delusion. The Talmud states that a person does not commit a sin unless he is overcome with a spirit of insanity (*Sotah* 3a). If it were not for this delusion, a person would not sin.

R' Shneur Zalman explains in *Tanya* that during the inquisition and similar oppressions, when Jews were forced to renounce their faith or be killed, many Jews who were not Torah observant chose to accept martyrdom rather than to deny G-d. He asks: Why did this devotion to G-d not cause them to observe His Torah? R' Shneur Zalman answers that every Jew wishes to have a relationship with G-d. A person may not understand that a violation of Torah distances him from G-d. He is living under a delusion that one can be close to G-d without observing the Torah. When he is asked to renounce G-d, this delusion is no longer effective, and he chooses to die rather than to sever his relationship with G-d.

Thus, even a sin due to temptation would not occur if the person were not deluded to believe that yielding to temptation would not affect his contact with G-d.

We can adjust properly to reality only to the degree that we have a correct perception of reality. A person suffering from a psychosis that causes him to be delusional and hear voices cannot function well in reality.

Delusions are extremely stubborn. It is easier to convince a normal person to consider the possibility that he might be dreaming and that everything he sees is a hallucination than to get a person suffering from paranoia to consider that the voices he hears are in his mind and are not being broadcast to him or that the FBI and CIA are plotting to kill him. The delusional thoughts that the *yetzer hara* plants in a person's mind are very difficult to resist.

This is the Baal Shem Tov's basis for explaining our prayer, "Compel our *yetzer hara* to be subservient to You." What are we asking of G-d? To make the *yetzer hara* urge us to do mitzvos? That is not its mission. Its duty is to tempt us to sin, and it is our duty to resist the temptation, but we cannot expect the *yetzer hara* to tell us to obey G-d.

The Baal Shem Tov answers, "G-d indeed created the *yetzer hara* to tempt us to sin. But if that is all it would do, we have the strength to resist temptation. However, the *yetzer hara* does not just tempt us with sin. It deludes us to think that what we wish to do is not a sin at all. In fact, it may even delude us to think that a particular sin is actually a mitzvah. That is how the serpent convinced Adam and Eve to eat from the Tree of Knowledge: if they would do so, then "they would be like angels, who know good and evil" (*Genesis* 3:5). Not only was the Tree of Knowledge not forbidden, the serpent argued, it was actually G-d's will that they partake of it, for certainly G-d would be pleased if they became like angels.

If the *yetzer hara* succeeds in deluding us, distorting our perception of reality and causing us to have a spirit of insanity, we are helpless. Therefore, we ask of G-d, "Compel the *yetzer hara* to be subservient to You," i.e., to do what it was created to do, to tempt us to sin, but do not allow it to delude us.

To defeat the *yetzer hara* we must be on the alert. We should be aware of its cunning, and that it tries to delude us. *Each time a sin is repeated, the delusion* (that it is permissible) *becomes more deeply entrenched (Moed Kattan* 27a). The Gaon of Vilna says, "Mastery over the *yetzer hara* is achieved not by forcibly controlling the urges for pleasure after one has allowed them to grow powerful, but by refusing to permit these drives to gain power at the start. At first, before habit has made a place for them in one's life and *before the soul has been corrupted* (deluded) *by the influence of evil,* all temptations to do evil are easily controlled" (*The Juggler and the King* p.43).

The Talmud says, "If this evil force contacts you, take it into the *Beis Midrash* (Torah study hall) (*Succah* 52b). Why? Because there we can have recourse to the works of halachah and to Torah authorities and can ascertain whether what the *yetzer hara* claims is true or false. We can have a "reality check" and defend ourselves against being deluded.

> *The yetzer hara never relents. R' Yisroel of Rizhin asked, "Why does the Talmud refer to the yetzer hara as an 'old and foolish king'? It is old, because it is as old as Creation. It is a king because it rules over so many people. But in what way is it foolish? On the contrary, the yetzer hara appears to be very sly and cunning.*
>
> *"But when I was imprisoned, the yetzer hara did not leave me. I said, 'No sane person wishes to be in prison. I had no choice. I was put in chains and dragged here. But no one forced you to come. If you came into prison of your own accord, you are indeed a fool.' "*

Although this is witticism, it is very true. There are no conditions when the *yetzer hara* departs from us. At times of joy or at times of sorrow, whether one is wealthy or poor, scholarly or unlearned, healthy or sick, the *yetzer hara* is always with us. This is why we must forever be on our guard.

Our struggle with the *yetzer hara* does not abate. R' Shneur Zalman states that when one of two wrestlers gains the upper hand, the other makes an increased effort to topple him. If we succeed in vanquishing the *yetzer hara* in one encounter, we should not be lulled into a false sense of security. It will try to attack us with even greater force.

But, we can triumph! We have the works of *mussar* and *chassidus* that teach us how to overcome the *yetzer hara*. We can stay in close contact with Torah scholars and halachic authorities who can guide us in resisting the wile of the *yetzer hara*. Above all, we are strengthened, supported and encouraged by the infinite power of G-d. The Talmudic statements, "Whoever comes to be purified will be assisted by G-d" (*Shabbos* 104a) and "Open for Me a passage the size of a needle's point, and I will open for you a portal like the doors of an arena" (*Shir HaShirim Rabbah* 5:3), insure us that if we initiate the process, G-d will surely help us bring it to a successful conclusion.